Contents

D0851558

WILD FLOWERS
OF FLORIDA

By Glenn Fleming, Pierre Genelle,
and Robert W. Long

Photographs by
Pierre Genelle and Glenn Fleming

Banyan Books, Inc.
Miami, Florida

Glenn Fleming, M.A., is Research Associate, University Her-barium, University of South Florida, Tampa; Pierre Genelle, B.A., is also Research Associate, University Herbarium, University of South Florida. The late Robert W. Long, Ph.D., was Professor of Botany and Director of the Herbarium of the University of South Florida.

Third printing, 1984
A co-publication of
Banyan Books Inc. and
Vanderbilt Press Inc.

Second printing, with revisions, 1979

Designed by Bernard Lipsky

Manufactured in the United States of America
Printed by Dynamic Litho, Miami, Florida

Library of Congress Cataloging in Publication Data

Fleming, Glenn, 1908 —
 Wild flowers of Florida.

 Bibliography: p.
 Includes index.
 1. Wild flowers—Florida—Identification.
I. Genelle, Pierre, 1911-   joint author. II. Long,
Robert W., 1927—   joint author. III. Title.
QK154.F56   582'.13'09759   76-43050
ISBN 0-916224-08-2

Illustration credits: Photos except p. 72 by the authors. Cover photograph and p. 72 by Walter Dawn. Cover illustration shows a field of zephyr lilies, *Zephyranthes atamosco* Adans., a species usually found along roadsides and in moist fields. These lilies bloom in spring.

Title page illustration of prairie iris by Linda Baumhardt. Diagrams pp. 10 and 11 by Priscilla Fawcett.

Preface

In writing this book we hope to enable Florida residents and visitors to become acquainted with a few of the more conspicuous wild flowers of the state. We have endeavored to include representative flowers from all the principal plant formations that occur in the state, but admittedly we have not been able to include all the species. Rather, we have tried to include those flowering plants that a casual observer may see along the roadsides, in the fields and marshes, or in similar places within natural areas.

The scientific name and common name are given for each plant. Scientific names are of universal application. No matter what language a wild flower book is written in, the scientific name, rendered in Latin, will always be the same for a given plant, even though the common name may differ. Although all authors do not agree about all aspects of naming plants, we have tried to use those names that appear to us to be correct according to the International Code of Botanical Nomenclature. We have, for the most part, used the same nomenclature adopted by Long and Lakela in their *A Flora of Tropical Florida*.

We have also included certain pertinent information about each species to aid in correct identification. The usual habitat for the species and the blooming time are given so that you may know where and when to look for a particular species.

Florida is a large state geographically, and we have an immense and abundant native plant life. We consider the flora to be one of our most precious natural heritages and one that deserves recognition and protection. The phenomenal growth of Florida in recent years has had a drastic effect on the vegetation, and development has destroyed and altered many areas formerly occupied by the native flora. We should all concern ourselves with helping to preserve what is left of our marvelous flora. Indiscriminate collecting and removal of native plants should be discouraged. Some of the plants we have included in this book are protected by state law and should never be taken. We owe it to generations yet unborn to help preserve this valuable natural resource.

Wild Flowers of Florida is a product of many years of studying Florida flora. Many persons, too many to mention here, have helped us to prepare this book. We are especially indebted to Dr. Olga Lakela, to whom his book is dedicated, for helping us over the years to become better acquainted with the Florida plants.

The Authors

Tampa, Florida, July 1976

Introduction

The native plant life of Florida is one of the most remarkable in the whole of the United States. Here there are over 3,000 species of plants, not including the many cultivated forms grown for horticultural purposes.

Geography and climate are primary reasons for Florida's unusual variety of plants. Most of the state is a peninsula extending from the temperate zone, where it borders Georgia and Alabama, south into the subtropical zone where it ends in Key West. Florida is, in effect, a bridge between the Appalachian and coastal plain flora of the temperate zone and the West Indian flora of the tropical zone. The location, coupled with a warm, moist, Antillean climate, has resulted in a rich, often luxuriant flora containing elements of both temperate and tropical vegetation. Soil also influences plant growth, and in most of Florida the surficial deposits are dominated by limestone derivatives and sands of oceanic origin. Many wild flowers are confined to certain kinds of soils, and this explains their often perplexing distributions within the state—while many species are adapted to sandy soils or to maritime soils, others are more frequently found near swamps or marshes. Knowing where to look for particular wild flowers is half the battle of finding them!

Plant Communities

In Florida we find a number of relatively well-marked kinds of plant communities or formations that differ from each other by the dominant or characteristic species that are found in them. Knowing which formation a particular wild flower belongs to can aid in knowing where to find it. For this reason, we include here a brief description of the principal plant formations of Florida and explain how they can be recognized.

Doubtless the most extensive plant formation is formed by the PINE FLATWOODS that are found throughout most of the state. These are often relatively open woodlands dominated by the longleaf pines—the slash pine *(Pinus elliottii)* and the southern longleaf pine *(Pinus palustris)*—and the understory shrub, the saw palmetto *(Serenoa repens)*. Isolated hardwood hammocks, swamps, and marshes are often scattered through this formation.

The PINE-SCRUB OAK FORESTS are also common in Florida, especially on well-drained uplands inland from the coastal areas, though many of these forests have been cleared for citrus groves. This formation is characterized by a number of species of oak *(Quercus sp.)* and slash pine. Most wild flowers found in the pine flatwoods and pine-scrub oak forests are temperate in origin.

A distinctive plant community that in general appearance resembles the pine-scrub oak forests is the SAND PINE-ROSEMARY SCRUB *(Pinus clausa, Ceratiola ericoides)*. This formation is well developed in central areas of the state, as well as in other isolated places, and is characterized by a number of interesting and unique wild flowers.

Still another characteristic plant formation in Florida is the MANGROVE ASSOCIATION, together with the usual bordering COASTAL MARSHES. The mangrove formation is dominated by the mangrove plants: the red mangrove *(Rhizophora mangle)*, the black mangrove *(Avicennia germinans)*, the white mangrove *(Laguncularia racemosa)*, and the buttonwood *(Conocarpus erecta)*. This community is of tropical origin and is found in tidal areas that vary from saline to brackish along the seacoast, principally in the southern half of the peninsula. The *coastal marshes* are especially well developed along the upper Florida west coast, but examples of this formation can be found in most coastal areas of the state. This formation is essentially a grassland dominated by such tall, coarse grasses as cordgrass *(Spartina sp.)* and such other salt-loving plants as sea purslane *(Sesuvium portulacastrum)* and glasswort *(Salicornia sp.)*.

Similar in appearance to the coastal marshes is the immense EVERGLADES FORMATION, a freshwater marsh that occupies most of the state south of Lake Okeechobee. Much of this area is a trackless wilderness of swamps, hammocks, swales, and ponds rich with wild flowers and containing a number of characteristic species. The formation is dominated by saw grass *(Cladium jamaicensis)*.

Closely related to the Everglades community are the SWAMP FORESTS that can be found in many parts of the state; the best representative is the Big Cypress Swamp of southern Florida. These forests are usually flooded by shallow water. Dominant species include bald cypress *(Taxodium distichum)*, southern willow *(Salix caroliniana)*, and dahoon *(Ilex cassine)*. This formation is also rich in wild flowers that may be found in bloom throughout most of the year.

Perhaps the most distinctive plant formation in Florida is the one found in the COASTAL DUNES and STRAND AREA. Sandy beaches and dunes are often narrow and offer a limited range for plants, but the floral composition of this formation is remarkably uniform and very similar to that found generally around the Caribbean basin. Some characteristic species found here are sea rocket *(Cakile lanceolata)*, sea grape *(Coccoloba uvifera)*, marsh elder *(Iva frutescens)*, and sea oats *(Uniola paniculata)*.

Origin of the Flora

Parts of the northern and central Florida, as well as much of the southeastern United States, have had continuous vegetation for a very long period of time. Large areas of southern Florida, however, have been submerged until relatively recent times. At the end of the last glaciation the seas rose to their present level, and the modern outline of Florida appeared.

Plant species migrated into Florida from three principal areas: (1) the southeastern coastal plain, Appalachia, and the temperate areas to the north; (2) the Antillean region, especially Cuba, Hispaniola, the Yucatán peninsula, and other areas of tropical America; and (3) islands that persisted during the time when most of the Floridan peninsula was submerged. The wild flowers, then, are derived from three dissimilar floras: the temperate flora, the tropical flora, and the central Florida highlands flora that includes a number of plants unique to Florida. In addition, during historical times a significant number of species have been introduced into Florida, have become naturalized, and have further enriched the flora.

Where and When to Look for Wild Flowers

The wild flower season can be said to begin in January, with the profusion and variety increasing through the spring and summer. Regardless of your location or the time of year, you are likely to find Florida wild flowers in bloom. Northern Florida and the Florida panhandle are more closely attuned to the seasonal variation found in Georgia and Alabama, but for most of Florida plants will be in flower from winter through fall. The best time for wild flowers, however, is spring and summer.

The white, sandy soils of central Florida may seem a sterile and unlikely place for wild flowers, but in fact this habitat supports a wide variety of plant life, including a number of species found only in Florida. Wet marshes and swamps, limestone ridges, beaches, and seasonally wet and high pinelands all have their own particular wild flowers.

Florida is unique in having a number of unusual plants that the collector may want to learn how to identify. These include such insect-catching species as the pitcher plants, sundews, butterworts, and bladderworts that have various kinds of traps enabling them to snare small animals. They are typically found growing in wet, peaty soils bordering swamps, or in shallow water. Another interesting group of plants are the bromeliads, including Spanish moss *(Tillandsia usneoides),* which grow attached to other plants and are called epiphytes. These do not ordinarily injure their hosts; rather they draw their nutrients from air and rain water. Some bromeliads produce strikingly beautiful flowers—for example, the air plant *Tillandsia fasciculata.*

Many bromeliads are mistaken for orchids. We do have a number of orchids, including some truly beautiful and often rare species. Many of these grow attached to trees and are fairly common, such as the Florida butterfly orchid *(Encyclia tampensis),* while others grow in the soil and are true terrestrial plants—for example, the curious ladies' tresses orchid *(Spiranthes cernua)*. Many of the orchid species are magnificent plants, but collectors should remember that they are protected by law and are not to be taken.

Still another group of interesting wild flowers includes such native cactus plants as the prickly pear cactus *(Opuntia compressa)*, often found growing in the white sand scrub or along the coastal strand. Other cacti belong to the genus *Cereus*, and some of these species are called tree cacti because of their upright or reclining cylindrical or angled stem bearing sharp spines. The stems may grow to be quite long.

Without doubt, however, the best place to go looking for wild flowers is right along the roadsides or in bordering old fields where the land has not been recently altered. A close inspection of these areas will almost certainly yield a number of species included in this book.

How to Use This Book

The wild flowers are arranged into four color groups: (1) white to green; (2) yellow to yellow orange; (3) pink to red or red orange; (4) purple to blue. Opposite each photograph is a brief description of the plant together with its common and scientific names, ecology, and other botanical information of interest. For the benefit of those who are familiar with the taxonomic order, a listing of species according to the family in which they are classified is included at the end of this introduction.

Although many wild flowers can be identified by using the color code in this book and then matching the plant with the appropriate photograph, it will be helpful to know the basic parts of the flower and to know how wild flowers can be accurately identified. We have made every effort to minimize the technical language that is often necessary to discuss plants scientifically, but a few terms are basic to understanding the differences between wild flowers, particularly those in the same family or having similar flower structure. You are urged to study the diagram in figure 1 in order to acquaint yourself with the meaning of the terms bract, sepal (calyx), petal (corolla), stamen, and pistil. The numbers and arrangement of these parts of the flower are important characteristics used to classify flowering plants.

Figure 2 shows the makeup of the "head" of a sea daisy, a typical member of the aster family. Note that the "flower" of the sea daisy is really a large number of very small flowers growing together on the same receptacle. Being able to recognize the structure will make it easier for you to identify wild flowers belonging to this large family.

No members of the grass or sedge families are included because they are not usually conspicuous flowering plants, and their identification involves special problems. This book will introduce you, however, to many interesting and beautiful members of Florida's rich wild flower flora.

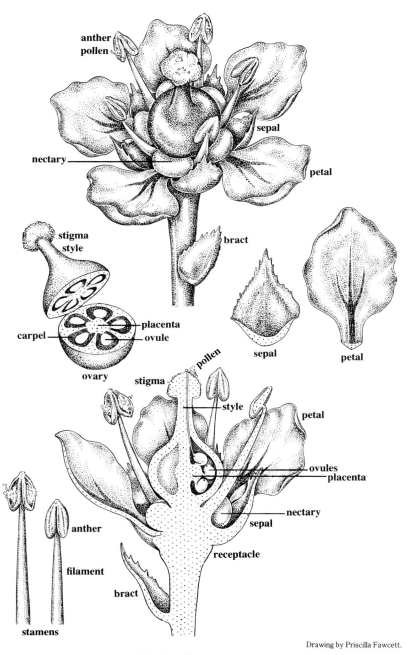

anther
pollen

sepal

nectary

petal

bract

stigma
style

placenta

carpel

ovule

ovary

sepal

petal

pollen

stigma

style

petal

ovules

placenta

nectary

sepal

receptacle

anther

filament

bract

stamens

Fig. 1—Parts of a flower.

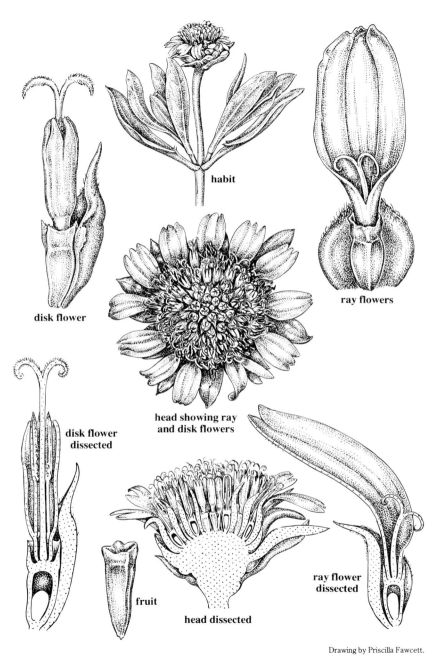

disk flower

habit

ray flowers

head showing ray
and disk flowers

disk flower
dissected

fruit

head dissected

ray flower
dissected

Drawing by Priscilla Fawcett.

Fig. 2—Diagram of a sea daisy, a typical aster family member.

Glossary

annual—a plant that lives one season or year.

axillary—in or arising from the angle on the upper side between a leaf and the stem.

bract—a small modified leaf under a head of flowers or a larger leaflike form around the flower that may be colored, as in poinsettia.

calyx – the sepals of a flower.

capsule – a dry fruit, usually splitting at maturity.

compound leaf—a leaf with two or more leaflets on a common leaf stalk.

cordate—heart shaped.

disk flower—a tubular flower, as in the head of a sunflower family member.

drupe—a fleshy fruit enclosing a seed with a stony covering.

ellipsoid – a football-shaped solid.

elliptic—oblong with regularly rounded ends.

endemic—a plant with one restricted area of distribution.

entire leaf—a leaf with smooth or even margins.

epiphyte—a plant growing upon another plant but deriving no nutrition from it.

glandular hairs—plant hairs that may be knobbed and sticky.

globose – nearly spherical in shape.

herb—a soft plant without woody structure.

ligule – a flat, straplike body; the strap-shaped part of a ray flower in the aster family.

linear—long and narrow, the margins parallel.

nodding—bending so that the flower tilts downward.

ovate—egg-shaped, with the broadest part below the middle.

ovoid – an egg-shaped solid.

pappus—specialized calyx of members of sunflower family; composed of bristles or scales.

perennial—a plant that continues to grow year after year from the same root base.

ray flower—a strap-shaped flower as in the head of a sunflower family member.

sepals—the outermost series of the flower parts.

shrub—a woody plant with several stems from the base.

simple leaf—a leaf with a single undivided blade per each leaf stalk.

smooth—without hairs.

spatulate – spoon or spatula shaped.

spike—an elongated, unbranched, tight mass of flowers.

stamen—the pollen-bearing unit of a flower.

tendril – an elongated twining segment of a leaf or branch by which a climbing plant clings to its support.

terminal flower—a flower borne at the tip of the stem.

terrestrial plant—a plant that lives in or grows from the soil.

valvate – opening by valves.

whorl—a number of leaves in a circular pattern around the stem.

wing – a thin membranous expansion of an organ as of a fruit; also the lateral petals of the flowers of the milkwort and pea families.

Phylogenetic Index

A phylogenetic listing of the families of the plants described in this book will be useful to the student of botany and will challenge the beginner to study similarities in a family group. The arrangement and sequence is that of the Engler and Prantl system and corresponds to that found in most modern manuals on flora. The genera and species are listed alphabetically under each family. The student will find most herbariums arranged in this manner.

Alismataceae Water Plantain Family
  Arrowhead *Sagittaria lancifolia* L.
Cyperaceae Sedge Family
  Star rush *Dichromena colorata* (L.) Hitchc.
Arecaceae (Palmae) Palm Family
  Saw palmetto *Serenoa repens* (Bartr.) Small
Araceae Arum Family
  Parson-in-the-pulpit *Arisaema triphyllum* (L.) Torr.
Eriocaulaceae Pipewort Family
  Hatpins *Eriocaulon decangulare* L.
Bromeliaceae Pineapple Family
  Wild pine *Tillandsia fasciculata* Sw.
  Spanish moss *Tillandsia usneoides* (L.) L.
Commelinaceae Spiderwort Family
  Dayflower *Commelina erecta* L.
  Roseling *Cuthbertia ornata* Small
Pontederiaceae Pickerelweed Family
  Water hyacinth *Eichhornia crassipes* (Mart.) Solms
  Pickerelweed *Pontederia cordata* L.
Agavaceae Agave Family
  Spanish daggar *Yucca aliofolia* L.
Haemodoraceae Bloodwort Family
  Redroot *Lachnanthes caroliniana* (Lam.) Dandy
Amaryllidaceae Amaryllis Family
  String lily *Crinum americanum* L.
  Yellow star grass *Hypoxis juncea* J. E. Smith
  Zephyr lily *Zephyranthes atamosco* Adans.
Iridaceae Iris Family
  Prairie iris *Iris hexagona* Walt. var. *savannarum* (Small) Foster
  Blue-eyed grass *Sisyrinchium atlanticum* Bicknell

Cannaceae Canna Family
  Golden canna *Canna flaccida* Salisb.
Orchidaceae Orchid Family
  Early grass pink *Calopogon barbatus* (Walt.) Ames
  Florida butterfly orchid *Encyclia tampensis* (Lindl.) Small
  Green-fly orchid *Epidendrum conopseum* R. Br.
  Michaux's orchid *Habenaria quinqueseta* (Michx.) A. A. Eaton
  Rose pogonia *Pogonia ophioglossoides* (L.) Ker.
  Ladies' tresses *Spiranthes cernua* (L.) L.C. Richard
  Lawn orchid *Zeuxine strateumatica* (L.) Schltr.
Saururaceae Lizard's Tail Family
  Lizard's tail *Saururus cernuus* L.
Polygonaceae Buckwheat Family
  Sea grape *Coccoloba uvifera* (L.) L.
  Jointweed *Polygonella polygama* (Vent.) Engelm. & Gray
  Smartweed *Polygonum hydropiperoides* Michx.
  Sorrel *Rumex hastatalus* Baldw.
Phytolaccaceae Pokeweed Family
  Pokeberry *Phytolacca americana* L.
  Rouge plant *Rivina humilis* L.
Aizoaceae Carpetweed Family
  Sea purslane *Sesuvium portulacastrum* L.
Portulacaceae Purslane Family
  Rose purslane *Portulaca pilosa* L.
Nymphaeaceae Water-Lily Family
  Yellow pond lily *Nuphar luteum* (L.) Sibth & Smith ssp. *macrophyllum* (Small) Beal
  White water lily *Nymphaea odorata* Ait.

Ranunculaceae Buttercup Family
Pine hyacinth *Clematis baldwinii* T & G
Magnoliaceae Magnolia Family
Southern magnolia *Magnolia grandiflora* L.
Sweet bay *Magnolia virginiana* L.
Annonaceae Custard Apple Family
Pawpaw *Asimina reticulata* Shuttlew. ex Chapm.
Papaveraceae Poppy Family
Yellow harlequin *Corydalis micrantha* (Engelm.) Gray
Brassicaceae (Cruciferae) Mustard Family
Sea rocket *Cakile lanceolata* (Willd.) O. E. Schulz
Rosaceae Rose Family
Chickasaw plum *Prunus angustifolia* Marsh.
Carolina laurelcherry *Prunus caroliniana* Ait.
Black cherry *Prunus serotina* Ehrh.
Swamp rose *Rosa palustris* Marsh.
Sand blackberry *Rubus cuneifolius* Pursh
Fabaceae (Leguminosae) Pea Family
Crab's eye *Abrus precatorius* L.
Cassia *Cassia coluteoides* Colladen
Partridge pea *Cassia chamaecrista* L.
Rabbit bells *Crotalaria spectabilis* Roth
Coral bean *Erythrina herbacea* L.
Milk pea *Galactia regularis* (L.) BSP.
Sensitive plant *Mimosa strigillosa* T. & G.
Sesban *Sesbania punicea* (Cav.) Benth.
Hoary pea *Tephrosia florida* (F. C. Dietr.) Wood
Cow pea *Vigna luteola* (Jacq.) Benth.
Meliaceae Mahogany Family
China berry *Melia azedarach* L.
Polygalaceae Milkwort Family
Yellow milkwort *Polygala lutea* L.
Yellow thimbles *Polygala nana* (Michx.) DC.
Milkwort *Polygala ramosa* Ell.
Yellow Batchelor's Button *Polygala rugelii* Shuttlew.
Anacardiaceae Sumac Family
Brazilian pepper tree *Schinus terebinthifolius* Raddi
Aquifoliaceae Holly Family
Dahoon *Ilex cassine* L.
Yaupon *Ilex vomitoria* Ait.
Malvaceae Mallow Family
Sida *Sida acuta* Burm.
Caesar weed *Urena lobata* L.
Theaceae Tea Family
Loblolly bay *Gordonia lasianthus* (L.) Ellis
Hypericaceae (Guttiferae) St. John's Wort Family

St. John's wort *Hypericum cistifolium* Lam.
Cistaceae Rock Rose Family
Frostweed *Helianthemum corymbosum* (Walt.) Michx.
Helianthemum nashii Britt.
Violaceae Violet Family
Florida violet *Viola affinis* LeConte
Primrose-leaved violet *Viola primulifolia* L.
Purple violet *Viola septemloba* LeConte
Turneraceae Turnera Family
Piriqueta *Piriqueta caroliniana* (Walt.) Urban
Cactaceae Cactus Family
Prickly pear *Opuntia compressa* (Salisb.) Macbride
Lythraceae Loosestrife Family
Loosestrife *Lythrum alatum* Pursh.
Rhizophoraceae Mangrove Family
Red mangrove *Rhizophora mangle* L.
Combretaceae Combretum Family
Buttonwood *Conocarpus erecta* L.
Myrtaceae Myrtle Family
Punk tree *Melaleuca quinquenervia* (Cav.) Blake
Melastomataceae Melastoma Family
Meadow beauty *Rhexia cubensis* Griseb.
Meadow beauty *Rhexia nashii* Small
Onagraceae Evening Primrose Family
False loosestrife *Ludwigia arcuata* Walt.
Primrose willow *Ludwigia peruviana* (L.) Hara
Evening primrose *Oenothera laciniata* Hill
Apiaceae (Umbilliferae) Celery Family
Button snakeroot *Eryngium aromaticum* Baldw.
Ericaceae Heath Family
Tarflower *Befaria racemosa* Vent.
Rusty lyonia *Lyonia ferruginea* (Walt.) Nutt.
Shiny lyonia *Lyonia lucida* (Lam.) K. Koch.
Sparkleberry *Vaccinium arboreum* Marsh.
Shiny blueberry *Vaccinium myrsinites* Lam.
Oleaceae Olive Family
Wild olive *Osmanthus americana* (L.) Gray
Loganiaceae Logania Family
Yellow jessamine *Gelsemium sempervirens* (L.) Ait. f.
Gentianaceae Gentian Family
Floating hearts *Nymphoides aquatica* (J. F. Gmel.) Kuntze
White marsh pink *Sabatia brevifolia* Raf.
Marsh pink *Sabatia grandiflora* (Gray) Small
Asclepiadaceae Milkweed Family
Milkweed *Asclepias feayi* Chapm.

Milkweed *Asclepias pedicellata* Walt.
Butterfly weed *Asclepias tuberosa* L. ssp. *rolfsii* (Britt.) Woodson
Convolvulaceae Morning-Glory Family
Morning glory *Ipomoea hederifolia* L.
Morning glory *Ipomoea trifida* (HBK.) G. Don
Polemoniaceae Phlox Family
Phlox *Phlox drummondii* Hook.
Hydrophyllaceae Waterleaf Family
Sky-flower *Hydrolea corymbosum* Macbride ex Ell.
Verbenaceae Verbena Family
Shrub verbena *Lantana camara* L.
Rose vervain *Verbena tenuisecta* Briq.
Vervain *Verbena tampensis* Nash
Avicenniaceae Black Mangrove Family
Black mangrove *Avicennia germinans* (L.) L.
Lamiaceae (Labiatea) Mint Family
Musky mint *Hyptis alata* (Raf.) Shinners
Lyre-leaved sage *Salvia lyrata* L.
Pennyroyal *Pilophlebis rigida* (Bartr. ex Benth.) Raf.
Skullcap *Scutellaria integrifolia* L.
Solanaceae Nightshade Family
Christmas berry *Lycium carolinianum* Walt.
Ground cherry *Physalis angulata* L.
Soda apple *Solanum ciliatum* Lam.
Potato tree *Solanum erianthum* D. Don
Scrophulariaceae Snapdragon Family
False foxglove *Agalinis fasciculata* (Ell.) Raf.
Fragrant bacopa *Bacopa caroliniana* (Walt.) Robinson
Bacopa *Bacopa monnieri* (L.) Pennell
Blue toadflax *Linaria canadensis* (L.) Dum.
Bignoniaceae Bignonia Family
Cross vine *Bignonia capreolata* L.
Trumpet creeper *Campsis radicans* (L.) Seem.
Lentibulariaceae Bladderwort Family
Violet butterwort *Pinguicula caerulea* Walt.
Yellow butterwort *Pinguicula lutea* Walt.
Bladderwort *Utricularia fibrosa* Walt.
Bladderwort *Utricularia inflata* Walt.
Acanthaceae Acanthus Family
Wild petunia *Ruellia caroliniensis* (J. F. Gmel.) Steud.
Rubiaceae Madder Family

Buttonbush *Cephalanthus occidentalis* L.
Buttonweed *Diodia virginiana* L.
Innocence *Hedyotis procumbens* (J. F. Gmel.) Fosberg
Caprifoliaceae Honeysuckle Family
Coral or trumpet honeysuckle *Lonicera sempervirens* L.
Southern elderberry *Sambucus simpsonii* Rehder
Black haw *Viburnum obovatum* Walt.
Cucurbitaceae Gourd Family
Creeping cucumber *Melothria pendula* L.
Wild balsam apple *Momordica charantia* L.
Campanulaceae Bluebell Family
Cardinal flower *Lobelia cardinalis* L.
Bay lobelia *Lobelia feayana* Gray
Glades lobelia *Lobelia glandulosa* Walt.
Asteraceae (Compositae) Aster Family
Aster *Aster caroliniensis* Walt.
Aster *Aster dumosus* L.
White-top aster *Aster reticulatus* Pursh
False willow *Baccharis angustifolia* Michx.
Salt bush *Baccharis dioica* Vahl
Groundsel tree *Baccharis glomeruliflora* Pers.
Groundsel tree *Baccharis halimifolia* L.
Green eyes *Berlandiera subacaulis* (Nutt.) Nutt.
Beggar-ticks *Bidens mitis* (Michx.) Sherff
Beggar-ticks *Bidens pilosa* L.
Sea daisy *Borrichia frutescens* (L.) DC.
Carphephorus *Carphephorus corymbosus* (Nutt.) T & G
Tickseed *Coreopsis leavenworthii* T & G
Yellowtop *Flaveria linearis* Lag.
Garberia *Garberia heterophylla* (Bartr.) Merr. & F. Harper
Narrow-leaved sunflower *Helianthus angustifolia* L.
Annual sunflower *Helianthus annuus* L.
Golden aster *Heterotheca scabrella* (T & G) R. W. Long
Rattlesnake weed *Hieracium megacephalon* Nash
Blazing star *Liatris chapmanii* T & G
Climbing hempweed *Mikania scandens* (L.) Willd.
Phoebanthus *Phoebanthus grandiflora* (T & G) Blake
False dandelion *Pyrrhopappus carolinianus* (Walt.) DC.
Goldenrod *Solidago fistulosa* Mill.
Small-headed goldenrod *Solidago microcephala* (Greene) Bush

Selected References

Baker, M. F. *Florida Wildflowers*. New York: Macmillan Co., 1926 (paperback reprint, 1972).

Brockman, C. F. *Trees of North America*. New York: Golden Press, 1968.

Burgis, D. S., and Orsenigo, J. R. *Florida Weeds,* Part One, Circular 331. Agricultural Extension Service. Gainesville: Univ. of Florida, 1969.

Bush, C. S., and Morton, J. F. *Native Trees and Plants for Florida Landscaping.* Bulletin 193, Dept. of Agriculture, Tallahassee, 1969.

Buswell, W. M. *Native Trees and Palms of South Florida.* Coral Gables: Univ. of Miami, Bull. 19 (6): 1-54.

Hawkes, A. D. *Guide to Plants of Everglades National Park.* Coral Gables: Tropic Isles Publishers, 1965.

Kingsbury, J. M. *Poisonous Plants of the United States and Canada.* Englewood Cliffs, N.J., Prentice-Hall, 1964.

Kurz, H., and Godfrey, R. K. *Trees of Northern Florida.* Gainesville: Univ. of Florida Press, 1962.

Long, R. W., and Lakela, O. *A Flora of Tropical Florida.* 1971. Rev. ed. Miami: Banyan Books, 1976.

Luer, C.A. *The Native Orchids of Florida.* Bronx, N.Y.: The New York Botanical Garden, 1972.

McGeachy, B. *Handbook of Florida Palms.* St. Petersburg: Great Outdoors Publishing Co., 1960.

Medsger, O. P. *Edible Wild Plants.* New York: Macmillan Co., 1939.

Morton, J. F. *500 Plants of South Florida.* Miami: E. A. Seemann Publishing Co., 1974.

Morton, J. F. *Wild Plants for Survival in South Florida.* Miami: Hurricane House, 1962.

Noble, M. *Florida Orchids.* Tallahassee: State Dept. of Agriculture, 1951.

Radford, A. E.; Ahles, H. E.; and Bell, C. R. *Manual of the Vascular Flora of the Carolinas.* Chapel Hill: Univ. of North Carolina Press, 1968.

Rickett, H. W. *Wild Flowers of the United States.* Volume Two, *The Southeastern States.* New York: McGraw-Hill Co., 1967.

Small, J. K. *Manual of the Southeastern Flora.* New York: Hafner Publishing Co., reprint 1972.

Walden, F. *A Dictionary of Trees.* St. Petersburg: Great Outdoors Publishing Co., 1963.

Weldon, L. W.; Blackburn, R. D.; and Harrison, D.S. *Common Aquatic Weeds.* Agricultural Handbook No. 352. Washington, D.C.: Supt. of Documents, 1969.

West, E., and Arnold, L. *The Native Trees of Florida.* Gainesville: Univ. of Florida Press, 1950.

WHITE WATER LILY *(Nymphaea odorata)*, water-lily family, is an aquatic herb with flat, orbicular leaves, 6 to 10 inches wide, that have smooth margins and dark purplish red undersides. White flowers, 3 to 6 inches wide, extend above the water 6 to 12 inches; they open in the morning and may close in late evening. Numerous yellow, ovate, thickish stamens add to the attractiveness of the blossoms, which appear from April to September. The fruit is berrylike with depressed sides. White water lilies are found in quiet pools, shallow lakes, and ditches; they range from Florida to Texas and south to Mexico.

FLOATING HEARTS *(Nymphoides aquatica)*, a member of the gentian family, is an aquatic herb with a single heart-shaped leaf and a flower cluster. Both are borne at the top of a single elongated stem: the glossy thick leaves are 2 to 6 inches across and purplish on the underside. The white flowers are ¾ inch wide and are found in clusters at the base of the leaf. The fruit is a hard, ellipsoidal capsule about ½ inch in length. Floating hearts is found in ponds, shallow lakes, and quiet waters, where it blooms from April to October; it extends along the coastal plain from Florida to Texas and north to New Jersey.

CLIMBING HEMPWEED *(Mikania scandens)*, aster family, is an herbaceous, smooth vine, with leaves 1 to 3 inches long varying from ovate to triangular to arrowhead shape. These leaves are opposite, wavy-edged, toothed, or plain. The pink or white flowers form flat-headed clumps at the ends of their stalks; they are in heads of four and have tufts of fine bristles. Fruits are ovate, angled, tufted seeds. Climbing hempweed is found in thickets and moist woods and along swamps; it blooms from June through September in wet grounds from Florida to Texas and Maine.

18

pure white

ARROWHEAD
(Sagittaria lancifolia), water plantain family, has leaves that may grow up to 6 feet tall under favorable conditions, but a height of 3 feet is more common. The name arrowhead derives from the arrow-shaped or lance-shaped leaves; wapato is an Indian name that refers to the starchy, potatolike tuber that may be used for food. Arrowhead grows in shallow freshwater and in moist soils. The leaves have milky juice, and long stalks topped with tapered blades 2 to 4 inches wide, while the flower, with its three white petals 1 to 2 inches wide, makes this plant one of the most conspicuous of those found in the ditches along Florida's highways. The fruits are about 2 inches wide and occur in heads of many compressed seeds. Arrowhead blooms throughout the year along the coastal plains of the Atlantic states.

STRING LILY

(Crinum americanum) belongs to the amaryllis family and is not a lily. The plant has a flat-topped cluster of five or more fragrant white flowers, 3 to 6 inches wide, at the top of a 4- to 32-inch stalk. These flowers have distinctive purple anthers resulting in a bloom of exquisite beauty. The basal, strap-shaped leaves, 2 to 4 feet long and 1½ to 2½ inches wide, have soft-toothed margins. The fruit is a three-lobed, roundish capsule 1½ inches wide. String lily grows in marshy areas and ditches on the coastal plains of Florida and to Texas and blooms in summer and sporadically throughout the year.

19

pure white

LOBLOLLY BAY *(Gordonia lasianthus),* a member of the tea family, grows to over 30 feet tall with dark gray, thick, roughened bark, its leaves are 4 to 5 inches long, elliptic, shiny, and dark evergreen; the five-petaled white flowers, silky on the back, are 3 inches wide and grow on long stalks from the axils of new leaves. The fruit, ¾ inch long, is an ovate, woody capsule that splits halfway into five parts. Loblolly bay grows in swamps, ditches, and bay heads and blooms from May to September; it ranges from central Florida west to Louisiana and north to North Carolina. The bark has been used for tanning leather.

INNOCENCE *(Hedyotis procumbens)*, madder family, forms mats of herbaceous, prostrate, creeping stems up to 1 foot long, with many small, white, four-lobed, funnel-shaped flowers. The roundish leaves are ½ inch long; the flowers are single at the tips of branches. Fruits are capsules about ⅛ inch long and somewhat hairy. Innocence blooms in spring and fall in sandy soils of the coastal plain from Florida to Louisiana and North Carolina; look for it in pinelands, along roadsides, at the edges of fields, and in neglected lawns.

PAWPAW
(Asimina reticulata), custard apple family, is a shrub about 4½ feet tall with cream-colored flowers 2 inches long that appear singly on the wood of the previous year before the new leaves emerge. The simple, oval to oblong, leathery leaves vary from 2 to 3 inches in length and are very hairy beneath; the whitish, nodding flowers have six petals and appear in groups of one to three along the stem. The fruit, about 2 inches long, is oblong and yellowish green. Pawpaw grows in sandy soil of low pinelands and is frequently seen in cleared areas such as power line rights-of-way, or along roadsides. It blooms in early spring in a showy display and is limited to Florida. The fruit is considered edible, but some individuals either are sensitive to contact with it or develop stomach upsets after eating it.

SPARKLEBERRY *(Vaccinium arboreum)*, heath family, is a small tree that grows up to 25 feet tall and has numerous white, fragrant, pendant, bell-shaped flowers, about ½ inch long, in short spikes. The bark is brown, smooth, and flakes off in large, thin, irregular plates; the persistent leaves are ½ to 2 inches long, alternate, shiny dark green above, and broadly elliptic. The shiny, black, globose fruit, about ¼ inch in diameter, is long-stalked and has purple flesh surrounding eight to ten bony seeds. Sparkleberry grows in hammocks and open woods and blooms in spring, with the fruits ripening in fall; it ranges from central Florida to Missouri, Virginia, and Texas.

SOUTHERN ELDERBERRY *(Sambucus simpsonii)*, honeysuckle family, is a shrub or small tree up to 10 feet tall, with white pith in the stem. The leaves are opposite and divided into five to nine leaflets, 1 to 3 inches long; the small white flowers form a lacy, compact cluster 4 to 6 inches wide. The berries are black and juicy and can be used to make jellies or wine. This species is found along roadsides, canal banks, or pond edges, where frequently it forms dense thickets; it blooms throughout the year and is the only elderberry found in Florida. Other elderberries occur in most parts of the U.S. but their leaves drop in winter and fresh, rapid growth appears in the spring.

BLACK HAW

(*Viburnum obovatum*), honeysuckle family, a shrub or low tree up to 15 feet tall, has many flattened clusters, 1 to 2 inches across, of small white flowers producing one of the early spring's beautiful roadside floral displays. The simple, opposite, leathery, shiny, dark green leaves, ½ to 2 inches long, are broadened upward; the fruit is a black, one-seeded drupe, about ¼ inch long, that ripens in the summer. This shrub grows in hammocks and margins of swamps along the coastal plain from Florida to Virginia.

GROUNDSEL TREE (*Baccharis halimifolia*), aster family, which occurs naturally along the Florida coast, is usually a shrub and may grow up to 12 feet tall. Nonflowering plants may be recognized by the leaves, about 2 inches long, simple, coarse-toothed, with bases wedge-shaped and tips pointed. The flowers are small and greenish in dense heads and appear in the fall on axillary stalks; male and female flowers grow on different plants. The white-haired seeds mature on the female plant and make it a handsome, silvery-tufted specimen suitable for shrubbery borders. Related species are *B. glomeruliflora,* with stalkless heads; false willow *(B. angustifolia),* with its narrowly linear leaves; and *B. dioica,* with spatula-shaped leaves, which is less showy and generally found closer to the salt marshes and coastal swamps. These plants range from the West Indies to Texas and North Carolina.

SEA ROCKET *(Cakile lanceolata),* a low fleshy herb that belongs to the mustard family, is a spreading plant, usually lying on the ground, with narrow leaves about 3 inches long. The distinctive feature is the pod, about 1 inch long, which has two parts, a small basal part and a large terminal, ovate part. The white flower is less than ⅓ inch long with four petals. Sea rocket is found on the coastal dunes and seashores of Florida and the Keys, where it blooms all year.

LIZARD'S TAIL

(Saururus cernuus), lizard's tail family, is a delightful freshwater herb that grows from 1½ to 3½ feet tall with drooping, curved spikes of tiny, white flowers. The alternate leaves are 3 to 4 inches long, aromatic, and ovate, or else lance-shaped with a cordate base and a sharp point; the flowers have no petals, but rather white stamens along an elongated stem. The fruit consists of three or four ovaries fused at the base. Lizard's tail blooms from April to September, principally in freshwater marshes, swamps, roadside ditches, or in moist soil; it ranges from Florida to Texas and north to New England, Minnesota, and Quebec. In the 18th century the roots were pounded into a pulp and, because of their healing qualities, applied to wounds and sores.

BUTTONWEED *(Diodia virginiana)*, madder family, is a reclining, perennial herb with weak, smooth or hairy stems about 3 feet long. The tubular, stalkless, four-lobed, white flowers are ¼ to ⅜ inch long, and are solitary or in threes per leaf axil. The fruit is a nutlet, less than ½ inch long, with two persistent, hairy sepals at the top. Buttonweed grows in moist sites, swamps, and stream beds, and blooms all year; it is found throughout Florida to Texas, New Jersey, and Missouri.

CHICKASAW PLUM *(Prunus angustifolia)*, rose family, grows to 9 feet tall and has reddish brown twigs with clusters of white flowers that appear before the new leaves. These flowers are ⅜ inch wide and occur in groups of two to four with thirteen to twenty stamens; the leaves are ¾ to 2 inches long, lance-shaped with sharp points, shiny above, and somewhat hairy beneath. Fruits are 2 to 4 inches long, oval, red or yellow, and edible. Chickasaw plum is found in sandy soil, edges of woods, thickets and fencerows, and neglected fields. It blooms in February and March and ranges from Florida to Nova Scotia.

HATPINS

(Eriocaulon decangulare), pipewort family, has single, whitish, semiglobose heads, about ¾ inch wide, at the ends of ten-ribbed stems 1 to 3 feet tall. The grasslike, stalkless leaves are 4 to 20 inches long and form a basal rosette, while the fruiting head has tiny transparent seeds. Hatpins grows abundantly in wet places and is conspicuous in moist roadside ditches; it blooms from February to November along the coastal plain from Florida to New Jersey. The heads make excellent dried flowers for winter bouquets.

25

pure white

SAND BLACKBERRY *(Rubus cuneifolius)*, rose family, is an arching shrub with many hooked or straight prickles. The stems may grow up to 6 feet tall and usually arch and recline on surrounding vegetation. The leaves have three to five leaflets on prickly stems, and they are densely white-hairy beneath. The flowers are up to an inch wide, the petals white; the fruit is black, dry and tasty. Sand blackberry grows in sandy woodlands and fields throughout the coastal plain from Florida to Alabama and northward. Look for the blossoms in March and the ripe fruits in late summer; the latter make good pie or jam.

BEGGAR-TICKS *(Bidens pilosa)*, aster family, is a very common, square-stemmed herb up to 3 feet tall that grows almost anywhere in sandy soils. The leaves are opposite, toothed and three-parted. The showy, white flower heads are seen all year. The blossoms have five white ray flowers on each head, with yellow disk flowers that form a bloom about 1 inch across and arise from the leaf axils on long stalks. The fruit is a dry, spindle-shaped seed with two barbed tips; these seeds stick to clothing and animals' fur, giving the name of beggar-ticks. Through this excellent method of seed dispersal, beggar-ticks can be found in all types of locations from Florida to Mexico, the West Indies, and Central America.

*pure
white*

STAR RUSH
(Dichromena colorata), sedge family, with its triangular stem and narrow leaf blades, grows up to 3 feet tall in wet areas, road ditches, and along edges of freshwater bodies and streams. The drooping bracts at the ends of the stems are white with long, narrow, tapering green tips. The flowers, ¼ inch or less long, occur as spikes in the center of the bracts; leaves grow up to 1½ feet long and are grasslike; the fruit is a tiny, dry, yellowish seed with a beak. Plants bloom from March to November in very wet areas; they range from Florida to Virginia, Texas, and Mexico.

MUSKY MINT

(Hyptis alata), mint family, is an herb up to 6 feet tall, clustered with flattish, oval heads of white flowers less than ½ inch long. The leaves are lance to egg-shaped, toothed, wedge-shaped at the base, and have fine wool on the underside. The fruit is a tiny ovoid nutlet. Musky mint blooms all year, weather permitting, and grows in moist pinelands, swamps, and hammocks from Florida to Texas, North Carolina, and the West Indies.

pure white

WHITE MARSH PINK *(Sabatia brevifolia)*, gentian family, is a much-branched, slender-stemmed herb 1 to 2 feet tall, with small whitish flowers at the ends of the branches. The narrow, opposite leaves are ½ to ¾ inch long; the petals, up to ½ inch long, have yellowish bases. The fruit is a small capsule about ⅛ inch long. White marsh pink is found in low wet ground, fields, and pinelands, where it grows with grasses about the same height; it blooms from March to December along the coastal plain from Florida to Alabama and Virginia. The pink species of marsh pink grow in sandy marshes and along swamp edges.

PRIMROSE-LEAVED VIOLET *(Viola primulifolia),* violet family, is a white-flowered violet with oval, smooth leaves that have either wedge-shaped or heart-shaped bases on long winged stalks. The three lower petals of the flower have brown purple veins; the capsule is green and contains tiny reddish brown seeds. This violet grows in meadows, moist open woods, marshes, and swamps and blooms from February to April from Florida to Texas and north to Minnesota.

LADIES' TRESSES

(Spiranthes cernua), orchid family, is one of the most common orchids that grow in the soil; it appears in damp rich soil and moist meadows. This slender herb, which grows up to 2 feet tall, has grasslike leaves that clasp the stalk; and its fragrant white flowers, about ½ inch long, are arranged in a graceful spiral around the upper one-third of the stalk. The fruit is a very small capsule. Ladies' tresses grows from Florida to Texas and north to Maine, and blooms from April to December. Orchids fall into two basic types. One, the epiphytic, grows on trees but is not a parasite, and has swollen, bulblike basal structures believed to store water. The roots, which hang in the air, have a corky, white substance that absorbs the water, and their nutrients come from the dirt and debris that fall on them. The second and more common group of orchids grows in the soil. All wild orchids are protected by law in the state of Florida and should not be picked.

SPANISH DAGGER

(Yucca aliofolia), agave family, produces a flowering stalk to 10 or more feet tall, with many drooping, cream-colored flowers 1½ to 2½ inches long. This shrubby plant has gray green, rigid, sharp-pointed leaves up to 2 feet long, and grows on coastal sand dunes and in sandy, dry, open pine woodlands. The fruit is a light brown nodding capsule 2 to 3 inches long; the blossoms are dependent on the yucca moth that brings about pollination. Yuccas supply fibers for a type of cordage, and the roots of some can be used to produce a soaplike lather for cleansing. Plants bloom in spring and summer on the coastal plain from Florida to Louisiana and North Carolina. They are frequently cultivated because of their showy blooms, but the sharp leaves limit the areas where they may be planted.

29

pure white

SWEET BAY *(Magnolia virginiana)*, magnolia family, is a tree up to 60 feet tall, with leathery, dark evergreen leaves, shiny above and silvery below. These leaves are 3 to 6 inches long, smooth-edged, and taper to a point; in the breeze they show their silvery undersurfaces. The flower is about 2 inches wide and not as spectacular as that of southern magnolia *(M. grandiflora)*, but it is a delightful, fragrant white blossom; the ten to twelve petals last but one day before turning brownish. The fruits appear in a conelike structure. Sweet bay blooms from April to October and is in swamps and wet woods along the coastal plain from Florida to Texas and Massachusetts.

SOUTHERN MAGNOLIA *(Magnolia grandiflora)*, magnolia family, is a tree with magnificent white flowers and may reach a height of 60 to 80 feet and a diameter of 2 to 3 feet. Its foliage, with leathery, evergreen leaves in umbrellalike clusters, forms a conical crown. The leaves are 4 to 9 inches long, elliptic or oval-shaped, persistent, and shiny above; they have a dense coat of brown or rusty colored hairs beneath, and the margins turn under somewhat. Flowers are 6 to 8 inches in diameter, solitary on short stalks at the ends of the branches; they are white, but turn creamy at maturity and are strongly fragrant. The conelike fruit is 3 to 5 inches long and releases from numerous small slits hard, brown, flattened, kidney-shaped seeds about ¾ inch long that are covered with a scarlet skin and hang from the cone by silken threads. This tree grows naturally in hammocks and swamps in central and northern Florida and is planted as an ornamental in southern Florida; it ranges along the coastal plain from central Florida to Texas and North Carolina and blooms in spring and early summer.

30
*cream
white*

WILD OLIVE
(Osmanthus americana), olive family, is a small tree with simple, opposite, shiny, evergreen leaves, 2 to 6 inches long. Flowering in March, the small blossoms perfume the air with a heavy, sweet fragrance; they are greenish white, funnel-shaped, and four-lobed and occur in dense clusters in the axils of the leaves. The fruit is a dark purple, fleshy drupe, ½ inch in diameter, one-seeded, and bitter. Wild olive grows in swamps or damp woods and ranges from Florida to Louisiana and Virginia.

CAROLINA LAURELCHERRY
(Prunus caroliniana), rose family, is a shrub or tree that grows up to 40 feet tall with evergreen, lance-shaped leaves 2 to 5 inches long. The short, drooping, cream white spikes of flowers are fragrant and have outwardly angled petals. Fruits are blackish drupes, ½ inch long, with a thin, dry layer of flesh over the seeds. This species blooms from February to May and ranges along the coastal plain from Florida to Texas and north to North Carolina. It grows on river banks and in hammocks; as a shrub it is sometimes used for hedges and windbreaks.

REDROOT *(Lachnanthes caroliniana)*, bloodwort family, is an herb up to 2½ feet tall with a stem that is smooth below and covered with long soft hairs toward the top. The root has a red sap, and the older species name *tinctoria* indicates it may have been used as a dye. The sword-shaped leaves are shorter than the stem and are greatly reduced higher on the stem; they have no hairs and sheathe the stem. The flowers are terminal, ½ inch wide, yellowish and densely clustered—because of the many hairs they appear white. The capsule is covered with long soft hairs and the tiny seeds are black and narrowly winged. Redroot grows in pine flatwoods, bogs, and hammocks along the coastal plain of Florida to Louisiana and Massachusetts, blooming in the summer.

LAWN ORCHID *(Zeuxine strateumatica)*, orchid family, is a slender, leafy plant 2 to 7 inches tall, tinged with brown or purple, with small white or yellowish flowers in a dense spike. Leaves are grasslike, overlapping to sheath the stem; flower petals, up to 1/5 inch long, are shorter than the light tan bracts; and the fruit is a capsule about ¼ inch long. Lawn orchids appear in lawns, along roadsides and hammock edges, and in wet fields; they bloom in late winter (or throughout the year in southern Florida) and are restricted to Florida and the warm parts of Asia. Appearance in lawns is often hailed as a harbinger of spring by those who live in central and northern Florida.

WHITE-TOP ASTER

(Aster reticulatus), aster family, is a 1 to 4 foot tall herb, with many blunt leaves 2 inches long, and terminal clusters of 1-inch-wide flower heads that have white rays and a yellow disk. Leaves are 1½ to 3½ inches long, elliptic or egg-shaped, with netted veins and finely toothed margins. The fruit is a tiny, hairy, dry seed. This aster grows in brackish marshes and low ground areas along the coastal plain from Florida to South Carolina and blooms in spring and summer. Two other common asters in our area have bluish ray flowers: *A. dumosus,* a slender plant found in dry areas, up to 3 feet tall with small heads; and *A. caroliniensis,* a climbing, vinelike plant, with stems that extend to 12 feet long and flower heads 2 inches across. This latter species makes a striking display when sprawled across a mound of vegetation.

PUNK TREE or CAJEPUT TREE
(Melaleuca quinquenervia), myrtle family, has soft, shaggy, thick bark. Leaves vary from 2 to 7 inches long and are simple, smooth-edged, and taper to a sharp point; cream-colored flowers form a cylindrical spike, 5 to 6 inches long, resembling a narrow bottle brush. Fruits are light brown capsules, about ¼ inch long, in persistent, spiked clusters near the ends of the branches. Naturalized from Australia, punk trees grow up to 20 feet tall or more in moist soil, cypress swamps, and hammocks; they bloom all year throughout Florida and are used extensively for hedgerows and windbreaks. Unfortunately, in the lower Florida Gulf Coast the plant has become a noxious pest in crowding out the native species of the area, and control measures are necessary to prevent its spread. Another genus often seen is *Callistemon* sp. R. Brown, the popular cultivated Bottlebrush, distinguished from *Melaleuca* by its bright red stamens.

33
cream white

SIDA *(Sida acuta)*, mallow family, an herbaceous shrub, grows to 2 or 3 feet tall with many smooth branches. The leaves are ½ to 3 inches long and have various shapes from lance to rhombic. The white or pale yellow flowers, ½ inch wide, may have a red base; they arise from the leaf axils with stalks longer than those of the leaf stem. The fruit splits into ten to twelve small, beaked, one-seeded divisions. Sida blooms all year in disturbed sites and along roadsides and ranges from Florida to Texas, Arizona, and North Carolina.

ZEPHYR LILY

(Zephyranthes atamosco), amaryllis family, is a lilylike plant with a large, white, funnel-shaped blossom that may be tinged with pink and is borne at the end of a stout stem about 1 foot tall. Plants grow in low, open pinelands and at swamp edges. The leaves are 4 to 10 inches long and arise from the base but may be inconspicuous. The flower is up to 3 inches long and has six separate petals tapering to slender tips that curve outward; the calyx, just below the petals, is papery and brown. The fruit, a three-lobed capsule, is depressed at the top. Zephyr lilies bloom in spring in Florida in moist areas. The bulbs were used by the Seminoles to cure toothache.

34

*off
white*

MILKWEED

(Asclepias feayi), milkweed family, has flat clusters of small, white flowers, each about ½ inch long, on the slender stalks, up to 1½ feet tall, that arise from the leaf axils. These flowers have a crown of special structures with slits to catch the legs of insects that then carry away pollen sacs to the next plant. Leaves are 1 to 4 inches long, very thin and narrow, opposite, and attached to the stem without stalks. The fruit is 4 inches long, narrow, spindle-shaped and filled with seeds with thick, silky hairs. Found only in the pinelands of central Florida, milkweed blooms in Florida from spring to fall. It is said to have been used by the Seminoles as a remedy for snakebite.

BUTTONBUSH

(Cephalanthus occidentalis), madder family, is usually found as a shrub, but may grow up to 25 feet tall. The plants have rounded, irregular crowns with stout, short branches. Leaves have blades 8 inches long, are opposite, entire, short-stalked, and somewhat oval-shaped; the white flowers are in dense, spherical heads that with their long, protruding, spikelike stamens resemble pincushions. The fruits form a round, compact ball of nutlets, up to 1 inch in diameter, giving rise to the name buttonbush. These shrubs grow in moist sites and margins of swamps and ponds. They bloom all year, with the major flowering occurring in early summer; they range from Florida to Minnesota, Mexico, and the West Indies.

JOINTWEED *(Polygonella polygama),* buckwheat family, is a woody-stemmed perennial 1 to 2 feet tall, usually much-branched. The lower leaves are 1 inch or less long, threadlike to narrowly spatula-shaped; the inflorescences, about 1 inch long, of tiny white or pinkish flowers are scattered along the ends of the numerous branches. Fruit is ovoid and tiny. Jointweed blooms in the summer and fall in sandy soils, pinelands, and scrub forests along the coastal plain from Florida to Virginia.

RUSTY LYONIA *(Lyonia ferruginea)*, heath family, an erect shrub or small tree, grows up to 15 feet tall. The evergreen leaves, 1¼ to 1¾ inches long, have rolled margins, a rusty undersurface, and are elliptic in shape; the small, white, globular flowers occur in flat-topped clusters that appear abundantly in the spring but sparingly thereafter. The fruit is a light brown dry capsule. Rusty lyonia is found in moist or dry, sandy and acid soils in the pinelands throughout Florida, along the coastal plain from Florida to South Carolina and in the West Indies and Mexico. Shiny lyonia *(L. lucida)* has the same range as rusty lyonia and frequently grows with it, but has shiny, smooth, flat leaves without a rusty undersurface. Its flowers are pink and urn-shaped.

36

*off
white*

TARFLOWER
(Befaria racemosa), heath family, is a showy and conspicuous shrub that may reach 5 or 6 feet tall, although it is usually shorter. The leaves are oval-shaped, about 1 to 2 inches long, rough hairy. The flowers are attractive, pinkish white, and fragrant on long, flowering, coarsely hairy stems. Many seeds are produced in dry capsules. Tarflower grows in sandy soils throughout the coastal plain area from Florida to Georgia. Look for plants to bloom in the spring in pine-scrub areas. Its nearest relatives are found in the tropics of America.

SHINY BLUEBERRY

(Vaccinium myrsinites), heath family, is an erect, much-branched shrub up to 2 feet tall, with small, glossy, green leaves and pink or white tubular or bell-shaped flowers. The leaves, less than 1 inch long, are oval or elliptic with bristly and glandular teeth; the flowers, about ¼ inch wide, occur in flat clusters. The berries are about ¼ inch wide, globular, and blue black. Shiny blueberry grows in sandy pinelands, open woods, and fields and blooms in spring in acid soils along the coastal plain from Florida to Louisiana and North Carolina.

POTATO TREE *(Solanum erianthum)*, nightshade family, has woody stems up to 9 feet tall and simple ovate leaves 4 to 12 inches long. Stems, flowers, and leaves are densely covered with short, soft, matted hairs. The inflorescence is flat-topped with white flowers, about ½ inch wide, and the fruit is a yellow, globose berry, 2/5 to 4/5 inch wide. This shrub blooms throughout the year in sandy soil in south Florida, West Indies, and tropical America.

BLACK CHERRY *(Prunus serotina)*, rose family, is a tree that may grow up to 100 feet tall with a trunk 4 to 5 feet in diameter. Twigs are smooth, slender, and gray to brown, while the leaves are 2 to 6 inches long, elliptic, simple, shiny, and dark green with paler undersides. The drooping white spikes of flowers, 4 to 6 inches long, make a striking display against a blue sky. Fruits are ½ inch wide, round, smooth, and nearly black; they ripen in May and are eaten by birds. Black cherry grows from Florida to Texas and north to North Dakota and Ontario and blooms in February and March; the larger trees have become scarce but smaller ones are found in hardwood hammocks and along roadsides. At one time the satiny, brown wood was used to manufacture furniture.

BUTTON SNAKEROOT *(Eryngium aromaticum)*, celery family, has spreading, reclining to suberect stems up to 2 feet long. The oblong leaves, 1 to 1½ inches long at the base of the plant, become smaller on the upper part of the stems; they are three- to five-parted, and each division is spine-tipped. The whitish to blue green, buttonlike, long-stalked flower heads, about ⅓ inch wide, arise from the leaf axils and are spiny-prickly. The fruit is a tiny granule. Button snakeroot blooms spring and summer and grows in glades, ditches, and bogs along the coastal plain from Florida to Georgia.

38

*off
white*

PARSON-IN-THE-PULPIT

(Arisaema triphyllum), arum family, has a green, cornucopialike sheath that rises up and droops down over a solid spike of white flowers. The plant with its three-parted leaves, 2½ to 4½ inches long, grows from a flattened, fleshy disk a few inches below the soil surface. The flowers are crowded around the basal portion of the fleshy spike; the drooping tip of the sheath is darker green than the cornucopia portion. Fruits are in red clusters, 1¼ to 2 inches long. Parson-in-the-pulpit grows in the deep shade of hammocks in rich mucky soil and may be seen along old woods' roads; it blooms in early spring in central and south Florida.

BUTTONWOOD *(Conocarpus erecta),* combretum family, is often called a mangrove. It attains a tree height of 60 feet but remains a shrub in many areas. The name refers to its purplish green, buttonlike fruits. Leaves are 1 to 4 inches long, leathery, evergreen, alternate, and may be clustered near the ends of the red brown twigs; when there are no fruits, the plant may be recognized by these twigs with their numerous lengthwise, raised lines. Flowers are small and greenish in dense spherical heads. Buttonwood occurs near saltwater areas on Florida's subtropical shores southward along the Keys and into tropical America. It is another of the shore-builders, its roots binding the shore and counteracting wave action. Buttonwood was used extensively in the last century by charcoal makers, who cut vast forests to supply their needs. There is also a "silverleaf" variety of buttonwood that occurs in southern Florida.

39

green
white

MICHAUX'S ORCHID
or LONG-HORNED ORCHID

(Habenaria quinqueseta), orchid family, is named for the botanist who first discovered and described it. The plant is a terrestrial orchid with stems from 8 to 20 inches tall and many whitish flowers, ¾ inch wide, arranged along a spikelike stalk. The spur of the flower is of varying lengths, but what distinguishes this species are the flower's five threadlike extensions that sweep downward and outward. Leaves are elliptic and diminish in size on the upper stem; capsules are ½ to ¾ inch long and are short-stalked. Michaux's orchid blooms in the fall in moist pinelands throughout Florida to Georgia and Texas, and other varieties of this species grow in Central and South America and Cuba.

40

green

SEA GRAPE *(Coccoloba uvifera),* buckwheat family, is a much-branched tree or shrub up to 45 feet tall. The leaves are 4 to 10 inches long, round or kidney-shaped, thick and heart-shaped at the base. The whitish flowers are stalked on spikes 4 to 10 inches long; the male flowers are clustered, but the female are solitary. The roundish, pale green to reddish or purple fruits are 1 inch in diameter. Sea grape blooms in spring or fall in coastal hammocks and dunes in the southern half of Florida and the Keys of Central America. The edible fruit is often used to make jelly.

BLACK MANGROVE *(Avicennia germinans)*, black mangrove family, may reach 60 feet but is usually smaller. Its complicated root system has numerous, short vertical branches called "pneumatophores" that are often covered with algae. Leaves are 2 to 4 inches long, opposite, leathery, shiny above and hairy beneath; flowers are white and downy. Fruits are about 1 inch long, green, downy, ovate, but with unequal, flattened sides. Black mangrove is one of the most common trees in the coastal swamps of southern Florida, where it grows along the sandy shorelines and in coastal hammocks. It blooms throughout the year (but most heavily in June and July) at the ends of new growth and ranges from Florida to Texas and south into tropical America and West Africa.

41

green

MILKWEED

(Asclepias pedicellata), milkweed family, is a slender, unbranched herb, 1½ feet tall, that bears a flat-topped clump of crown-shaped, greenish to cream-colored flowers, about ½ inch long, on stalks ¾ to 1 inch long. This plant is distinct from other milkweeds because the petals turn upward around the corona or crown rather than downward. The grasslike to lance-ovate, fine-haired leaves, 1 to 2 inches long, are opposite and stalkless. This milkweed blooms in spring and summer in the pinewoods of Florida to North Carolina.

GREEN-FLY ORCHID *(Epidendrum conopseum)*, orchid family, is a common epiphytic orchid without pseudobulbs that often grows in association with resurrection fern *(Polypodium polypodioides)*, which may hide it from view. The gray green flowers are ½ inch wide and grow on stems 2 to 8 inches long. The elliptical, smooth leaves are 1 to 3 inches long; usually not more than three appear per plant; their color is often purplish, depending on the amount of sunlight they receive. The fruit is an ellipsoid capsule, ½ to 1 inch long, that hangs downward. This orchid blooms from January to August in moist areas on many kinds of trees and in cypress swamps from Tampa and Ft. Lauderdale to Louisiana and North Carolina. Green-fly orchid is the most common epiphytic orchid in Florida found north of the range of the Florida butterfly orchid.

42
green

FLORIDA BUTTERFLY ORCHID *(Encyclia tampensis)*, orchid family, is one of the most beautiful epiphytic orchids, as well as the most common—it can be found in nearly any forest or hammock in southern Florida. It has dark green pseudobulbs, about 1 inch in diameter, which have papery sheaths at the base; the one to three leaves are 2 to 8 inches long and resemble thick, stiff grass leaves. Flower stalks up to 30 inches long bear three to forty yellow brown flowers about 1 inch wide; the lower lip is white with a strikingly brilliant crimson spot that can vary greatly in size and intensity. The fruit is a hanging capsule ¾ inch long. This orchid ranges from north central Florida to the Keys and the Bahama Islands with a blooming period of spring to summer. Florida butterfly orchid was first collected near Tampa in 1846 by the famous botanist, Dr. John Torrey, who sent it to England—thus the species name *tampensis*.

PHOEBANTHUS

(Phoebanthus grandiflora), aster family, is limited to central Florida. The perennial, rough, erect herb, up to 3 feet tall, grows from horizontal tubers in sandy soil. The single, straight stem may have a few branches, but frequently its single bright yellow flower head faces directly upward. The leaves, 1 to 2½ inches long, are entire, narrow, and parallel sided. Flower heads are conspicuous: the sixteen to twenty ray florets have ligules about 1½ inches long. The disk is nearly 1 inch wide. Phoebanthus grows in sandy soil of the pinelands and oak scrub of central Florida and blooms throughout the summer.

43
yellow

YELLOW BACHELOR'S BUTTON

(Polygala rugelii), milkwort family, has a single, dense, lemon yellow cluster of flowers at the top of each 10- to 30-inch stem. The wings of the individual flowers in the cluster are ⅓ inch long, much greater than those of the other yellow polygalas. The lower spatulate leaves are in a tuft and somewhat fleshy, the upper ones are thinner and narrower, the broader half outward. The fruit is tiny. Yellow bachelor's button is endemic to peninsular Florida and can be found in moist low ground, swamps, and low pinelands; it blooms from spring to fall. The Seminoles drank a hot infusion of this plant for snakebite.

RABBIT BELLS
(Crotolaria spectabilis), pea family, is an erect annual that grows to 3 feet tall. The undivided leaves are 3 to 6 inches long; the handsome, yellow flowers are 1 inch wide and have variegated dark lines. The pods, each over an inch long, are almost cylindric; when mature they become dark brown and develop seeds that rattle when the pod is shaken. Rabbit bells prefers sandy soil and is frequent along Florida roadsides. It is an introduced species that blooms from February to December with a range of Florida into the tropics.

FALSE LOOSESTRIFE *(Ludwigia arcuata)*, evening primrose family, is a purslanelike creeping perennial with numerous fleshy leaves and conspicuous flowers on axillary stalks longer than the leaves. Leaves have no stalks, are entire and narrow; flowers are about ½ inch across, yellow, and have four petals and four stamens. The fruit is a somewhat curved capsule, less than ½ inch long. False loosestrife blooms in spring and fall in moist soils of the coastal plain from Florida to Virginia.

TICKSEED *(Coreopsis leavenworthii),* aster family, with its rounded clump of yellow ray flowers and brown disk, decorates the roadsides, open fields, and pinelands of Florida for many months. It is a perennial up to 3 feet tall and has thin, branched stems with leaves divided into threadlike segments. Flowers are about 1 inch across and occur in numerous heads; the fruit is a seed about ⅛ inch long with two barbed tips at the end. This species of tickseed grows only in Florida, usually in moist areas. The plants bloom all year, but most heavily in spring and summer.

45
yellow

BLADDERWORT
(Utricularia inflata), bladderwort family, is an aquatic herb that grows up to 6 inches tall and floats on its basal whorl of inflated leaves 2 to 3 inches long. These submerged leaves are finely divided and have bladders that entrap small aquatic animals. The yellow flowers, about 1 inch wide, have a lower lip with three lobes and are borne in clusters of three or four at the ends of the stalks. The fruit is a capsule. Bladderwort grows in shallow, quiet water of ponds and ditches and blooms from late March to November. It ranges from the coastal plain of Florida to Texas and north to New Jersey.

NARROW-LEAVED SUNFLOWER *(Helianthus angustifolius),* aster family, has many flowers and rough, hairy, narrow leaves; the ray flowers and dark-colored disk are typical of the sunflowers. This perennial herb grows in moist ground or sometimes in sandy areas. It has a stem 3 to 6 feet tall with alternate leaves 3 to 6 inches long. The ray flowers are 1½ inches long and bright yellow, and the purple disk is about ½ inch wide. Fruits form a compact head of typical sunflower seeds. This species blooms from July to October in moist pinelands, woods, and prairies from Florida to Texas, Missouri, and New York.

GOLDEN CANNA
(Canna flaccida), canna family, our only known species of wild canna, grows in swamps and wet woods at heights up to 5 feet tall. The pale green, smooth-edged leaves may be up to 3 feet long. Large, bright yellow flowers form a showy cluster at the top of the stem; the blossoms, which may be 4 inches long by 3 inches wide, occur in groups of three and four, and the three petals form an erect tube with their ends curving downward. All the flower parts are petallike, except for one stamen that bears the pollen. The mature capsule is three-cornered and bristly and contains globular, brown seeds that gave rise to the common name of "Indian-shot" for the plant. Golden canna begins to bloom in April and may continue to bloom all year in southern Florida. It may be found in swamps, marshes, and flooded pinelands from Florida north to Mississippi and North Carolina.

GOLDEN ASTER

(Heterotheca scabrella), aster family, one of the more showy golden asters, is a yellow-flowered herb about 3 feet tall. The numerous basal leaves are spatula-shaped and rough to the touch; the heads have many tiny flowers, nearly 1 inch across, that form clusters at the ends of glandular, hairy stems. The fruit is ⅛ inch long and is a dry seed. Golden aster flourishes in sandy soils and blooms from August to January along the coastal plain from Florida to Mississippi.

BLADDERWORT *(Utricularia fibrosa)*, bladderwort family, an aquatic herb, grows with its stems submersed and creeping on the bottom in shallow water and some of the leaves rootlike. The flower stalk lacks floats but many of the leaves are bladder-bearing; this stalk is 4 to 16 inches long and has two to six yellow flowers, usually three. The flower is about 3/5 inch long and has a spur about as long as the lower lip. The numerous leaves have blades two or three times forking and reforking into two equal parts. Tiny aquatic animals are trapped in the valvate bladders and digested. Bladderwort blooms in spring and fall in pineland ponds and slow-moving streams on the coastal plain from Florida to Mississippi and New York.

CASSIA *(Cassia coluteoides),* pea family, is a shrub 5 feet or less tall. The three to four pairs of leaflets, 3/5 to 1¼ inches long, are broader upward and pitted on the lower surface, and a gland occurs between the lowest pair of leaflets. Cassia flowers are irregular with one or two petals larger than the others; the ten stamens are unequal in size, and only seven are perfect. The long, yellow inflorescences are from the upper leaf axils. The legumes or pods, 2½ to 6 inches long and about ½ inch wide, are curved and have a blunt tip, while the seeds, 1/5 inch long, are olive brown and slightly pitted. This cassia blooms all year along canal banks and in mangrove borders in south Florida to the West Indies. It is often cultivated in the milder areas of Florida.

48

yellow

RATTLESNAKE WEED *(Hieracium megacephalon),* aster family, is a milky-juiced herb with a stem 2 feet tall and covered with purple hair. The plant has basal, hairy, purplish-veined leaves and yellow flowers produced in flattish heads at the ends of many branches. The leaves are 2 to 6 inches long, mostly basal, and rather oval-shaped; the flowering heads are made up of strap-shaped flowers with the outer ones blooming first. The fruits are dry seeds with tufts of soft, brownish hairs about ½ inch long; the ripened head of these seeds forms a dandelionlike sphere. Rattlesnake weed grows in dry, sandy soils along roadsides, in open fields, and in neglected areas and pinelands. Plants bloom from spring to fall and are common from Florida to Maine and Nebraska.

PIRIQUETA

(Piriqueta caroliniana), turnera family, an herb, grows up to 8 to 15 inches tall with hairy stems that usually bear a single yellow flower, 1 inch across, in the leaf axils. The ovate to lanceolate leaves are 1 to 3 inches long and are entire to occasionally toothed; the fruit is a round, green capsule about ½ inch long. Piriqueta blooms from midwinter to summer as the season permits but wilts almost instantly when picked. It grows in dry sites on sandy soil from Florida to the Carolinas.

EVENING PRIMROSE *(Oenothera laciniata),* evening primrose family, opens its yellow flowers in late afternoon, but the blossoms become copper-colored and wither by noon of the following day. The leaves are 1 to 1½ inches long, cut into many segments, and sharply tipped at the ends; the flower, in the leaf axils, is about 1 inch across and is in four parts; the fruit, about 1 inch long, is a narrow, cylindric capsule. A low-spreading plant, evening primrose is found in sandy areas along roadsides and in open fields. It blooms throughout the year with a range of Florida to Mississippi and New Jersey on the coastal plain and south into Mexico.

YELLOW THIMBLES

(Polygala nana), milkwort family, is a low herb, 1 to 5 inches tall, with thickish, somewhat spoon-shaped leaves. Leaf blades are light green, spatula-shaped, shorter than the flower stalks. The flower clusters are 1 to 2 inches long and form heads that are borne singly at the ends of the stems; these heads suggest four to ten green yellow thimbles with no leaves. The fruit is a capsule about 1/16 inch wide; seeds are of the same length and each has a curved beak. Look for yellow thimbles in the low, moist pinelands, where it blooms in late winter and throughout the growing season along the coastal plain from Florida to Louisiana and South Carolina. Milkworts are thought to increase the production of milk in cows.

COW PEA *(Vigna luteola)*, pea family, climbs over the surrounding vegetation or forms tangles along the ground. Leaves are pinnately divided into three lance-shaped leaflets, each one ⅛ to 1 inch long; the pale yellow bloom has an upper petal, 1 inch wide, which is much wider than the length of the flower. The narrow downcurved seed pods are up to 4 inches long with several seeds that incurve on both surfaces. Cow pea grows in moist waste places, woods, marshes, and along beaches from Florida to Texas, and to the West Indies, Central America, and South America. It blooms throughout the year.

50

yellow

RED MANGROVE *(Rhizophora mangle),* mangrove family, may be a shrub or tree from 4 to 75 feet tall. Its stout aerial roots give it the appearance of standing on the tips of its arching branches at the outer edge of shores. Leaves are 2 to 6 inches long, leathery, opposite, and simple; flowers are ½ to ¾ inch in diameter, have four yellow petals, and are produced in clusters of two or three on long stalks. The brownish, cone-shaped fruits are about 1 inch long initially, but elongate to 6 or more inches and contain a young seedling that will root immediately when it falls on muddy soil. Mangroves retard erosion and extend shorelines along the coasts of subtropical and tropical areas of the world. In Florida red mangrove can be found in shallow water or the exposed edges of mangrove forests that border the estuaries and coastline.

FALSE DANDELION
(Pyrrhopappus carolinianus), aster family, can be observed in bloom only in the morning because the brilliant yellow blossom is usually closed by noon. This herb has erect stems from 1 to 3 feet tall with mostly basal, deeply cut leaves 4 to 10 inches long. The dandelionlike heads, about 2 inches across, are at the ends of the flower stalks well above the leaves. Fruits are small dry seeds with tan tufts of hairs at the upper ends. False dandelion blooms irregularly throughout the year but is most conspicuous in the early spring. Plants can be found along highway shoulders, old fields, and waste places of the coastal plain from Florida to South Carolina.

SPANISH MOSS *(Tillandsia usneoides),* pineapple family, is a festoonlike, silver gray, many-branched, elongate plant that hangs from tree branches. A rootless plant, it merely uses the tree for support and may be seen from almost any roadside in Florida. Leaves are 1 to 3 inches long, threadlike, and covered with scales; flowers are small, yellow and greenish, and single from the leaf axils, with petals that curve upward. The fruit is a dry, light brown capsule ½ to ¾ inch long. Spanish moss blooms from April to November along the coastal plain from Florida to Texas and Virginia and south through the West Indies, Mexico, and South America. Until the mid-1930s the plant was gathered and "debarked," leaving a black inner thread resembling horsehair that was used to stuff upholstery. It belongs to the pineapple family and to the same genus as the wild pines.

MILKWORT
(Polygala ramosa), milkwort family, is a bright yellow-flowered herb, 4 to 20 inches tall, that prefers damp locations. The flowers, in dense spikes, form a branching inflorescence, from 1 to 6 inches across, at the top of the almost leafless stem; the basal leaves, 1 inch long, are lance-shaped or ovate with the broader part toward the tip. The seeds are tiny and covered with short hairs. Milkwort blooms from July to September in damp fields and pinelands along the coastal plain from Florida to Texas and New Jersey.

PRICKLY PEAR *(Opuntia compressa)*, cactus family, is a low, branching cactus 1 to 2 feet tall, somewhat erect, with thick, enlarged, oval-shaped, flattened joints armed with single spines. Leaves are very small, scalelike, and deciduous, with spines about 1½ inches long; the yellow flowers are 1½ to 2¼ inches long, contain many stamens, and are borne at the upper edge of the joints. The berry is 1 to 2 inches long, purplish or red, and full of seeds; Indians ate these berries, drying some like figs for later use. Prickly pear grows in sandy pinelands and blooms in late spring and summer; the bright flowers wither in a day. It ranges from Dixie County south along the coast of Florida.

CREEPING CUCUMBER *(Melothria pendula)*, gourd family, is an herbaceous, creeping or climbing vine with simple tendrils. Leaves, 1 to 2 inches wide, have thin blades, usually heart-shaped or angled, on bristly stalks. The bell-shaped, five-lobed yellow flowers are less than ⅓ inch across; the male (staminate) flowers are clustered, but the female (pistillate) flowers are solitary. The ripe fruit is a dark purple berry, ½ to 1 inch long, resembling a tiny watermelon while still green. Creeping cucumber blooms through the year in low ground, hammocks, and thickets from Florida to Texas and north to Virginia and Missouri.

YELLOW STAR GRASS

(Hypoxis juncea), amaryllis family, has bright yellow, six-pointed stars at the end of slender, flowering stems, 2 to 10 inches tall. Not a grass but a member of the amaryllis family, it is common in pine flatwoods, in open sandy fields, and in mowed power line rights-of-way. The threadlike leaves, which may be 3 to 8 inches tall, grow from the base of the plant; flowers are ½ to 1 inch across, hairy and green outside, one or two on a stem. Fruits are ellipsoid capsules with very tiny seeds. Yellow star grass blooms from February to September and grows along the coastal plain from Florida to North Carolina.

YELLOW BUTTERWORT *(Pinguicula lutea),* bladderwort family, is a yellow-flowered perennial that grows up to 1½ feet tall. The stem rises from a rosette of sticky, insect-catching leaves that curl inward; the terminal, bell-shaped flower, ¾ to 1½ inches wide, has a spur and five unequal petal lobes. The fruit is a capsule that opens irregularly. Yellow butterwort blooms from March to mid-June; it grows in low pinelands, on wet roadsides, and along ditches from Florida to North Carolina to Louisiana. The word *pinguicula* means "little fat one," alluding to the greasy leaves. The leaves of European species have been used to thicken milk.

BEGGAR-TICKS *(Bidens mitis),* a member of the aster family, grows up to 3 feet tall and has a many-flowered yellow head, 1 to 2 inches wide, with deeply cleft leaves. The several rays, ½ to 1 inch long, are strap-shaped and bright yellow. The leaf blades, 3 to 4 inches long, are three- to five-divided; each segment is linear or narrowly lance-shaped, entire or rough-edged. Beggar-ticks blooms all year. It frequently appears in large masses in damp meadows or on the borders of lakes, ponds, and wet hammocks from Florida to Mississippi and Virginia.

YELLOW HARLEQUIN

(Corydalis micrantha), poppy family, is a tender, spreading herb 4 to 12 inches tall with highly dissected leaves. Its flowers are pale yellow with the outer petal having a small crest; each flower is ½ inch long with its spur on the upper lip, placed so that its stalk is halfway between the base and tip of the blossom. The capsule, about ¾ inch long, consists of a series of bulges that contain the seeds. Yellow harlequin grows along roadsides, in citrus groves, and in fields, where it is closely associated with fume root *(Fumaria officionales);* it blooms from March to April and ranges from Florida to Texas and north to South Dakota and Virginia.

SEA DAISY *(Borrichia frutescens)*, aster family, is a seashore shrub up to 3 feet tall. The heads are usually solitary, many-flowered, with yellow rays; the disk is 3/5 inch or less wide, the rays, 2/5 inch or less long. The bracts of the flower head spread apart or curve downward. The opposite, greyish, short-haired, aromatic leaves, up to 3 inches long, are succulent and widest toward the end with a tiny projection at the tip; the dry one-seeded fruit is four-angled with a short four-toothed pappus. Sea daisy blooms in spring and summer along sea beaches, mangrove areas, and salt marshes from Florida to Texas and Virginia and south to the West Indies and Mexico.

56

yellow

FROSTWEED

(Helianthemum corymbosum), rock rose family, is an erect herb up to 1 foot tall with fine, short-haired stems and leaves and bright yellow flowers 1 inch wide at the top. The leaves are narrowly elliptic to oval, dark above and pale beneath; the flowers are in a dense, somewhat flattened cluster. The fruit, 1/8 inch long, is a many-seeded, dry capsule. Although most blossoms appear in March and April, frostweed blooms throughout the year. It grows in dry, sandy soil of uncultivated fields or roadsides and in pinelands and ranges along the coastal plain from Florida to Mississippi and to North Carolina. *Helianthemum nashii* has the same distribution as *H. corymbosum;* however, its blossoms are scattered along the stem instead of being in a cluster at the top.

ST. JOHN'S WORT

(Hypericum cistifolium), St. John's wort family, is a woody plant 1 to 3 feet tall with narrow leaves and bright yellow flowers in a flat-headed terminal arrangement. The leaves are 1 to 3 inches long and narrowly elliptic; the flowers have wedge-shaped petals up to ¼ inch long and many yellow stamens; and the fruit, ⅛ inch long, is a three-lobed, globose capsule. St. John's wort grows along pond and lake edges and river banks and in pinelands and wet areas and blooms from May to August from Florida to Georgia and Mississippi. The name St. John's wort (wort means plant) is tied to many superstitions surrounding St. John the Baptist. At one time this plant was used as a remedy for wounds.

SMALL-HEADED GOLDENROD *(Solidago microcephala)*, aster family, has small golden yellow heads arranged in a rounded mass of blossoms at the top of multiple branched stems 2 to 3 feet tall; each head has ten to seventeen tiny flowers. The slender, smooth, green leaves are 1 to 2½ inches long. Fruits consist of small black seeds, each with a tuft of hairs. This goldenrod is found throughout Florida's sandy pinelands; it blooms in late summer and fall and forms golden masses. Goldenrod is found from Florida to Mississippi and New Jersey. However, none of these relatives provides the same mass of solid color as does this species.

57

yellow

GREEN EYES *(Berlandiera subacaulis)*, aster family, is a perennial with thickened roots up to 2 inches in diameter. It has stiff-haired stems ½ to 1½ feet tall. Leaves are 2 to 6 inches long and deeply cleft; flowers are nodding, solitary, 1-inch-wide heads with eight to twelve rays and numerous yellow green disk flowers. The fruit is a hairy seed about 3/16 inch long, dry and ovoid-shaped. Green eyes grows in sandy soil along road shoulders and edges of woods, in neglected lawns, and in dry pinelands. It blooms abundantly in central Florida all year and is limited to Florida.

YELLOWTOP *(Flaveria linearis)*, aster family, is a much branched herb, 10 to 30 inches tall, with yellow heads in a flat compact, arrangement—the heads have a single ray flower and four to eight disk flowers in loosely grouped clusters. The smooth leaves are 2 to 4 inches long, entire and narrow, and the tiny fruits are dry seeds about 1/16 inch long. Yellowtop is found near the coast in hammocks and pinelands and along roadsides in Florida, the West Indies, and Mexico. It is often the most conspicuous plant in bloom in late September and October along salt marsh areas; however, blooming is infrequent the rest of the year. It is seen often by fishermen.

PRIMROSE WILLOW *(Ludwigia peruviana),* evening primrose family, has a woody base with tender stems that grow up to 6 feet tall and yellow flowers 2 inches across. The dark green leaves are 3 to 6 inches long, oval, and pointed with smooth edges. The flowers are solitary from the axils of the upper leaves; flower parts are in fours, with four large petals that drop at the touch and eight stamens. The capsule is about 1 inch long, stout, and four-sided. Growing in moist soils along ditches, canal banks, swamp edges, and ponds. Primrose willow is the most conspicuous and attractive of all this group in Florida. It ranges through Florida, Mexico, and tropical America and blooms all year. A number of other species of primrose willow grow in similar areas, but they are small and lack the attractiveness of *L. peruviana.*

59

yellow

YELLOW POND LILY *(Nuphar luteum* ssp. *macrophyllum),* water-lily family, is a water lily with lance-ovate, smooth, heart-shaped leaves that are 8 to 16 inches long and stand partially or entirely above the water or else float. The roundish, cuplike flowers are 1¼ to 2 inches wide and bright yellow within; the anthers are larger then the dull red filaments. The fruit, 1⅜ inches long, is somewhat globose. This lily grows profusely from strong, horizontal roots and may cover the entire pond. It blooms from May to October in ponds, marshes, and sluggish streams and ranges from Florida to Texas, Massachusetts, and Minnesota.

GOLDENROD

(Solidago fistulosa), aster family, has a large, loose, flower cluster, hairy stems and rough, clasping leaves. It grows to 3 or 4 feet tall and is found in sunny, moist, sandy areas. Many oval leaves, 2 to 3 inches long, tend to clasp the stem, while flowers are borne in groups of small heads in tapering, branched clusters that tend to arch downward. The fruit is a tiny, hairy seed. Goldenrod blooms in summer and fall in pinelands and hammocks along the coastal plain of Florida and southern Georgia.

SAW PALMETTO *(Serenoa repens)* differs from other members of the palm family because its stems frequently are branched. These stems, up to 20 feet long, creep, strongly rooted on the underside, and turn upward a few feet at the ends. The leafstalk is saw-toothed, three-sided, and fibrous on the edges at the base; leaf blades are fan-shaped to 3 feet wide, of circular outline, and divided handlike (palmately) into segments shallowly split at the tips. The three-petaled, yellowish white flowers are about ¼ inch long and form an inflorescence 1 to 3 feet long. The oval drupe, ⅔ to 1 inch long, is juicy, edible, and yellow, turning blackish when fully ripe. The fruits were an important food for Florida Indians; the stems are now a source of tannic acid, and the fragrant flowers a source of honey. Saw palmetto blooms in spring and summer in hammocks, coastal dunes, pinelands, and sandy soils from Florida to North Carolina.

YELLOW JESSAMINE *(Gelsemium sempervirens)*, logania family, is a woody, evergreen, perennial vine up to 20 feet long. In spring it is showy with its yellow, fragrant, tubular flowers, about 1 inch long, five-lobed, and clustered in the leaf axils or solitary. The opposite leaves, about 2 inches long, have short stems and are entire and lance-shaped; the fruit capsule is ¼ to ½ inch long, oblong, and short-beaked. Found in wild areas, fencerows, and woods' edges, climbing on trees or other objects, yellow jessamine blooms in winter and spring in low ground and hammocks from Florida to Virginia, Tennessee, and Arkansas. The plant contains alkaloids related to strychnine, making it poisonous to all animals.

PARTRIDGE PEA *(Cassia chamaecrista)*, pea family, is a showy spreading annual with finely divided leaves and yellow flowers. The blossom is over 1 inch long, but is not pealike; rather it has unequal petals, each with a purple spot at the base. The flowers also have long protruding, curving anthers that enhance their attractiveness. All Cassia species have one or more glands on the leaf stalk, and the size, shape, number, and position of these glands distinguish one Cassia from another: the partridge pea's leaf has ten to fifteen or more pairs of leaflets up to 4/5 inch long and ⅛ inch wide. The fruit is a pod covered with short hairs. Partridge pea can be seen all summer on hillsides, in open woods and sandy fields and along ditches from Florida to Texas, Kansas, Mississippi, and Minnesota.

ANNUAL SUNFLOWER

(Helianthus annuus), aster family, is an annual erect herb up to 6 feet tall, branched, more or less hairy, with a large flat head that nods and is made up of yellow ray flowers and gold to brown disk flowers. Leaves are 2 to 12 inches long, hairy, dark green, and toothed, while the fruit is a dry seed, ¼ to ¾ inch long, with a gray and white striped outer shell. This sunflower grows in cultivated grounds, waste places, and fields, along roadsides and dry plains, and blooms from April to November in Florida. It is found in almost all of the U.S. and is spread from bird feeders in Florida.

62

yellow
orange

WILD BALSAM APPLE

(Momordica charantia) is a member of the gourd family. A creeping annual herb with tendrils, it can be recognized by its warty, bright yellow or orange berry 1 to 2 inches long. The vines grow up to 20 feet long in sandy soil and may completely cover an area or thicket. The leaves are five- to seven-lobed; the flowers are yellow. When the berries split open the dark seeds and red flesh are most attractive and are a favorite food for birds. Flowering begins in May, fruiting in June or July to November. Wild balsam apple grows in all sandy parts of the coastal plain and ranges west to Texas and south to the West Indies and tropical America.

BUTTERFLY WEED *(Asclepias tuberosa* ssp. *rolfsii)*, milkweed family, is one of the showiest milkweeds, 1 to 2 feet tall, with orange or reddish flat-topped clusters of flowers at the ends of the branches. The hairy leaves are 2½ to 4 inches long, borne singly, and are narrow and pointed with very short or no leaf stalks. This species lacks milky juice. The flower is deeply cleft into five petals or lobes, at the junction of which rise five cups to form the crown that is characteristic of most milkweeds. The erect seed pods are 2 to 6 inches long. Butterfly weed grows in sandy soil, pineland areas, and along road rights-of-way. It blooms from March to October and ranges from Florida to New Hampshire and westward to Arizona, where it may be of a different subspecies. The plant has a deep tough root reputed to be a cure for pleurisy—thus its alternate common name of pleurisy root.

63

orange

YELLOW MILKWORT
(Polygala lutea), milkwort family, is a low plant that occurs in a cluster of leaves with stalked, orange flowers, and grows from 4 to 15 inches tall. The rather fleshy, light gray green leaves are 2 to 3 inches long and grow in a whorl at the base, bright, compact flowers form a cylinder, 1 to 2 inches long, at the ends of the stems; and the fruit is a capsule 1/16 inch long, plump and hairy. Milkwort grows in moist and sandy soils of fields and pinelands from Florida to Louisiana and New York and blooms from May to October. The name milkwort refers to the belief that the eating of the plant (wort means plant) by cows would increase their production of milk.

MILK PEA *(Galactia regularis),* pea family, is a much-branched perennial vine that may either lie on the ground or climb, has divided leaves 2 to 3 inches long, with purple flowers on a stalk about as long as the leaves. The three leaflets, ½ to 1½ inches long, are oval-shaped with tiny points at their tips. The flowers are ½ inch long, appear at the tips of the stems, and nod. The pod is flat; the halves twist spirally when mature, which releases the seeds. Milk pea grows in pinelands and oak scrub areas and dry fields: it blooms from June to November in mid-Florida and all year farther south, ranging along the coastal plain of Florida north to Georgia and Kansas and south to the West Indies.

SHRUB VERBENA
(Lantana camara), verbena family, is a showy, strong-scented shrub with flowers varying from pink to yellow, orange, and red. It reaches 3 to 5 feet in height and has square stems with weak prickles. Leaves are 2 to 5 inches long, opposite, toothed, rough, and aromatic; flowers are axillary and in flat-topped, dense heads; the fruit, ¼ inch in diameter, is a green blue or black fleshy drupe. Flourishing in fields, along ditches, and in fencerows, shrub verbena blooms all year in pinelands along the coastal plain from Florida to Georgia and Texas and south through tropical America. The plant is poisonous to sheep and cattle.

ROSE PURSLANE

(Portulaca pilosa), purslane family, is a prostrate, many-branched, fleshy-leaved annual that grows in sandy soils and has tufts of white hairs in the leaf axils. The thick leaves are ½ to ¾ inch long and almost cylindrical; the rose pink flowers, borne at the ends of the stems, are almost ½ inch across, with short stalks and bright yellow stamens. The fruit is a dry capsule, 3/16 inch long, whose top half pops off, revealing black seeds. Purslane blooms from spring to fall on the coastal plain from Florida to Texas and Georgia. The yellow purslane has small, fleshy, spatula-shaped leaves, no hair tufts in the leaf axils, yellow flowers, and is also found in Florida.

MORNING GLORY *(Ipomoea trifida)*, morning-glory family, is a lilac-flowered, perennial, twining herb that grows in sandy and dry soil. The leaves are 1 to 2 inches long, oval, either entire or three-lobed, and heart-shaped at the base. The three to ten flowers are 1 to 2 inches wide, 2 to 4 inches long, purplish, with a deep purple throat and a flaring lip. They are borne in groups in the axils of the leaves. The fruit is a dry capsule, pubescent at the top. Morning glory grows over surrounding vegetation, or sometimes trails on the ground; it blooms irregularly all year from central Florida to Louisiana and Texas.

65

pink

SWAMP ROSE *(Rosa palustris),* rose family, is a typical wild rose that grows up to 6 feet tall in swamp areas. Its stems, which may be reddish, have pairs of short, curved prickles, flattened at the base. The leaves are divided into seven leaflets, 1 to 2½ inches long, with fine saw-toothed edges, dark green above, pale beneath; the blades are either elliptic with pointed ends or lance-shaped. The pink flowers, about 2 inches across, occur singly or in twos and threes. The mature fruit is about ½ inch broad, almost globular and covered with glandular stiff hairs—the seeds are found at the bottom of this false fruit or hip. Swamp rose blooms in the spring and ranges from north central Florida to Minnesota.

MEADOW BEAUTY
(Rhexia cubensis), melastoma family, is distinguished by the glandular hairs that appear on the stem, at the base of the flower, and on the urn-shaped fruit capsule. It has the same attractive purplish, four-petaled flower as many other species of meadow beauty; this flower is 1 to 2 inches across and has long, curved stamens. Leaves are about 1½ inches long, narrow, and one-veined; the fruit is ½ to ¾ inch long with gland-tipped hairs and lance-shaped teeth on its lip. Blooms appear in spring and continue sparsely all year along the edges of swamps, pools, and in moist pinelands from Florida to North Carolina, Tennessee, and Louisiana.

VERVAIN

(Verbena tampensis), verbena family, is a showy herb 1 to 2 feet tall, with purple flowers in elongate or flat clusters; each flower of the cluster is about ½ inch long. The leaves are ¾ inches long, sharply toothed or lobed, elliptic or egg-shaped. Fruits are composed of four nutlets, ⅛ inch long. Vervain blooms in spring and fall and is found only in peninsular Florida in sandy soil of hammocks and open areas of woods.

MARSH PINK *(Sabatia grandiflora),* gentian family, is an erect, slender herb up to 3 feet tall that grows at the edges of ponds and ditches or in low pinelands. The upper leaves are 1 to 3 inches long and threadlike; the deep rose-colored flowers, about 2 inches across, grow at the ends of the stems and have five petals and a yellow eye. The fruit is a capsule about ½ inch long. Marsh pink blooms from March to November; it is restricted to peninsular Florida, but is one of our common wild flowers.

SENSITIVE PLANT *(Mimosa strigillosa)*, pea family, has sensitive leaves that fold up at the slightest touch. Its prostrate stems, with their rough, rigid hairs, spread along the ground bearing leaves divided into five to eight divisions that are further divided into many pairs of small leaflets. The tiny flowers are deep pink, crowded into oblong heads about 1 inch long at the ends of long stalks that arise from the leaf axils. Pods are 1 inch long and ⅜ inch wide, rough-haired, and one-to-four-jointed. This plant blooms from April to November and grows in damp soil in pinelands and hammocks and along stream banks and roadsides on the coastal plain from Florida to Georgia and Texas. Sensitive plant may be mistaken for sensitive briar, a sprawling, prickly plant with rose pink flowers in globose heads.

68

pink

EARLY GRASS PINK
(Calopogon barbatus), orchid family, is one of the earliest orchids to bloom in Florida. It reaches a height of ½ to 1½ feet, has only one or two grasslike leaves, 4 to 8 inches tall, and no more than five flowers at the end of the stem. These magenta flowers are up to ¾ inch long and open in rapid succession. Fruit is a beaked capsule about ⅜ inch long. Grass pink blooms in early spring from Florida to North Carolina; look for it in acid meadows, swamps, and low pinelands along old roads. This species is a good example of a terrestrial or ground orchid.

MEADOW BEAUTY

(Rhexia nashii), melastoma family, is one of a number of species of *Rhexia* that well deserve the name meadow beauty. It has attractive lavender to rose purple flowers with long, gracefully curving, yellow stamens and urn-shaped fruits. The stem is from ½ to 2 feet tall with flowers at the ends of axillary stalks. The opposite leaves, about 2 inches long, are lance-shaped without stalks and taper to a point. The hairless fruit, about ½ inch long, has narrow teeth on the lip. The plants bloom from May to October and often can be found in rich, moist soil and along ditches. They grow in all parts of Florida and extend to Louisiana and Virginia.

SMARTWEED *(Polygonum hydropiperoides)*, buckwheat family, is a semierect, perennial herb up to 3 feet tall. Long roots that develop many slender stems often give rise to a large clump of pink inflorescences, 2 inches or less long, with many stalkless flowers, ⅛ inch long, formed by white, green, or pink calyces. The leaves are narrow to lance-shaped, 2 to 5 inches long; the dry, one-seeded fruit is less than ⅛ inch long. Smartweed grows in swamps or moist places from mid-Florida to Texas and northward to Ontario and blooms all year.

ROSELING *(Cuthbertia ornata)*, spiderwort family, is a delicate, slender herb that grows in clumps of narrow, green leaves in open, sandy areas. These leaves are up to 1 foot tall, erect, slender, grasslike, and grow from roots that are copiously covered with long, soft hairs. The terminal clusters of pink flowers, about 1¼ inches wide, have centers of pink-haired stamens and three spreading, crinkly edged petals. The globular capsule is about ⅛ inch long. Roseling grows only in peninsular Florida, where it blooms from spring to fall in palmetto scrub, oak, and pine areas.

CAESAR WEED
(Urena lobata), a member of the mallow family, is a hairy-stemmed shrub up to 9 feet tall. Leaves are 3 to 6 inches long, oval with shallow lobes, and with fine hairs beneath; flowers are about ¾ inch long, rose or pink, and are borne in the axils of the leaves. The mature fruit, about ½ inch across, is brown, has five segments, and is flattened and covered with stiff spines that will stick to clothing. Plants bloom all year and fruits are persistent. Caesar weed grows in various soils, but chiefly in waste places and along roadsides; it ranges from Florida to the tropical areas of the Americas and Asia. Fiber can be obtained from the bark, and the flowers are said to have medicinal value.

ROSE POGONIA

(*Pogonia ophioglossoides*), orchid family, is a terrestrial, erect orchid 3 to 14 inches tall, with a single elliptic-ovate leaf, 1 to 4 inches long, halfway up the stem. The pink or rose flowers are about 1 inch long, usually one to three at the top of a round, greenish stem that is purple below. The lip is crested and fringed with a dark red beard that adds greatly to its attractiveness. Rose pogonia grows in marshes from south central Florida to Newfoundland and west to Texas; in Florida, it blooms in early spring.

SEA PURSLANE (*Sesuvium portulacastrum*), carpetweed family, is a fleshy herb found near seashores that sprawls to form a mat with branches up to 6 feet long. The fleshy leaves, ½ to 2 inches long, are broadest above the middle; the single, pink, stalked flower, about 4/5 inch long, has sepals with hornlike appendages. The fruit is ovoid, about ⅜ inch long. Sea purslane blooms all year on beaches and coastal dunes from Florida to North Carolina and southward to the West Indies, Mexico, and Central America. It is one of our most common seashore plants.

71

pink

CORAL BEAN

(Erythrina herbacea), pea family, a shrub, may grow 5 to 20 feet tall. The leaves are long-stalked with three triangular or arrowhead-shaped leaflets, 1 to 3 inches long. The scarlet, elongated inflorescences, up to 20 inches long, appear before the leaves, creating a bright flame in the coastal hammocks. The broad, upper petal of the red flower is notched at the end and may be up to 2 inches long; wing petals are ½ inch long and heart-shaped. The legume or pod, up to 4 inches long, is blackish, constricted between the seeds, and opens in the fall to reveal bright red seeds, ½ inch wide. These beans are hard enough to be used as beads; however, they are reputed to be poisonous. The blossoms appear in spring and summer in hammocks and pinelands along the coastal plain of Florida to Texas and North Carolina.

Photo by Walter Dawn.

72
red

CHRISTMAS BERRY *(Lycium carolinianum),* nightshade family, is a much-branched shrub, up to 6 feet tall, with many smooth, narrow, entire, fleshy leaves less than 1 inch long. The axillary flowers, about ¼ inch long, are blue or lilac, but much less conspicuous than the bright red berries, which are egg-shaped and about ½ inch across. Christmas berry blooms all year in hammocks, shell mounds, and coastal areas that flood with salt water from Florida to Texas to South Carolina.

BRAZILIAN PEPPER *(Schinus terebinthifolius),* sumac family, a good example of an introduced tropical plant that has escaped and successfully adapted to Florida, grows up to 9 feet tall and has arching branches. The leaves have three to eleven leaflets, each 1 to 2 inches long; the small white flowers appear in drooping clusters in the spring and summer, while attractive bright red or orange berrylike fruits that mature in late fall and early winter are often used for Christmas decorations. In late winter birds eat the berries and appear to become drunk from them; however, it may be that the fruits have not fermented but are slightly toxic. This species grows well throughout peninsular Florida, and is found in a wide variety of places, such as mangrove associations, hammocks, pinelands, and old fields. It often crowds out other plants and in many places is becoming undesirable—eradication measures may be called for unless some control is exercised.

CARDINAL FLOWER
(Lobelia cardinalis), bluebell family, the only lobelia species with red flowers, is an herbaceous perennial that grows 2 to 4 feet tall. The flowers, up to 2 inches long, have three sharp, lance-shaped lower lobes and two upper lobes that spread horizontally and are broader toward the tips. The conspicuously bracted, mostly one-sided inflorescence extends along the upper stem above the alternate, rough-edged, pointed-elliptic leaves, 1 to 3 inches long. The capsule is almost globular with a short beak. Cardinal flower blooms from July to September in wet soil along streams and in swamps and wet woods from mid-Florida to Texas and Quebec. There are few more brilliantly colored flowers in Florida.

PHLOX *(Phlox drummondii)*, phlox family, has showy, terminal, flower clusters of red, purple, or white that often form large, brightly colored patches along roadsides and in neglected fields. It is the annual phlox of our gardens. The flowers are about 1 inch wide and tubular below; in the wild they are typically rose red. The leaves are up to 3 inches long, opposite, and broad toward the base of the stem. Both stem and leaves are sticky with gland-tipped hairs. The fruit is an ovoid capsule. Phlox blooms from April to July in waste places and fields and ranges from Florida to Texas and the Carolinas.

WILD PINE
(Tillandsia fasciculata), pineapple family, is an air plant or bromeliad, with roots exposed to the air, but it is not parasitic. Except for Spanish moss, it is the most common bromeliad in Florida. The gray green plant, 1 to 2 feet tall, has stiff, curved, tapering leaves. Flower stalks extend above the leaves and bear red, green, or yellow bracts; the petals are violet and the fruit is a brown capsule that splits open when mature. Wild pine usually grows on cypress trees. There are a number of species of *Tillandsia* in Florida and they range into the West Indies, Mexico, and South America; this species of wild pine blooms from April to October.

SESBAN

(Sesbania punicea), pea family, has showy, orange red flowers that hang in large attention-getting clusters. The plant is a shrub with many-divided, drooping, dark green leaves; the number of leaflets on each leaf varies from twelve to forty. The colorful, pealike flowers are about 1 inch across, while the fruit is a papery, ridged pod, 2½ to 3½ inches long. Sesban blooms from April to November along hedge rows, ditch edges, roadsides, and waste places, along the coastal plain from Florida to Louisiana. It is attractive enough to deserve cultivation.

DAHOON *(Ilex cassine)*, holly family, grows to a tree height of 30 feet, but is usually seen as a shrub, often used in yards in Florida because of its red berries and shiny, dark evergreen leaves. The leaves, 2 to 4 inches long, have smooth edges with a few teeth toward the tip; the flowers, about ⅛ inch wide, occur along the stems, with male and female flowers on different plants. The fruits, ¼ inch wide, show along the stems between the leaves and remain there for months unless eaten by birds. They contain four to eight pale brown seeds. Dahoon blooms heavily in April and May and more lightly the rest of the year; it grows in swamps, along stream banks, and in hammocks, in acid soils of the coastal plain from Florida to Louisiana and Virginia. Early settlers used the leaves of dahoon to brew a tea; yerba maté of South America is a close relative and is a favorite hot beverage.

CRAB'S EYE
(Abrus precatorius), pea family, is a woody vine 10 to 20 feet long that climbs on other plants and grows in sandy waste areas and pinelands that have been partially cleared. The most striking feature of the plant is the pod, about 1½ inches long, which when mature splits open to reveal glossy, scarlet seeds, each with a jet black lower one-third. The reddish flowers, ½ inch long, occur in clusters, while the divided leaves may have 20 to 30 leaflets about ½ inch long. The fruit is oblong to rectangular and contains three to five seeds. Crab's eye blooms from May to September from Central Florida to the West Indies and Mexico. The seeds have been used to make necklaces and rosaries, but this is a dangerous practice: one seed, if thoroughly chewed, is sufficient to kill an adult human being.

76
red

ROUGE PLANT
(Rivina humilis), pokeweed family, is a straggly herb that grows to 3 feet tall and is often found in sandy areas with citrus trees. The leaves are 1 to 4 inches long and taper to a sharp point. The white flowers appear on an elongated stalk and produce such attractive bright red berries that the plant is sometimes grown as an ornamental. Rouge plant blooms all year in areas not recently cultivated, along the coastal plain from Florida to Texas and south into South America. It has become a weed of wide distribution in tropical climates.

YAUPON *(Ilex vomitoria),* holly family, a shrub or tree, grows up to 24 feet tall. The leaves are 1 inch long, tough, scalloped, elliptic to ovate, dark green above, pale below; the white flowers, ¼ inch wide, bloom in the spring, but the numerous, round, red drupes, less than ½ inch wide, appear in winter. This shrub grows in sandy hammocks, sand dunes, and hills along the coastal plain of Florida, Texas, Arkansas and Virginia. The leaves contain caffeine and were used by the aborigines to prepare a black, bitter brew for ceremonial activities. Drunk only by the men, it usually acted as an emetic; if a man could retain the concoction he was entrusted with important missions.

POKEBERRY *(Phytolacca americana),* pokeberry family, is a large, stout herb with reddish stems that grow from 5 to 10 feet tall. Leaves are 4 to 12 inches long, widest toward the base and tapering to a point; they are relished by many insect larvae, so that the plant often has a ragged appearance. The greenish, white, or pink flowers are arranged on a flowering stalk 6 to 8 inches long, and the purple black berries are flattened globes highly prized as food by birds. The large root is very poisonous, but the young shoots may be used as greens. Pokeberry grows in moist woods and rich soil; it blooms throughout the year from Florida to Texas and north to Maine and Minnesota. Painters and Indians have used the berry juice as a pigment.

MORNING GLORY

(Ipomoea hederifolia), morning-glory family, is a twining, herbaceous vine with ovate leaves, 1½ to 4 inches long, that come to a gradual point and have a somewhat heart-shaped base. The scarlet or orange flower, ¾ inch wide, has a tube about ¾ to 1½ inches long and may be solitary or in flat-topped clusters in the leaf axils. The fruit is a four-seeded capsule. This vine can be found in fields and waste places from Florida to Arizona and north to New England; it blooms from July to October.

78
red

CROSS VINE

(Bignonia capreolata), bignonia family, is a smooth-stemmed, woody vine that grows up to 30 feet in length. Leaves are divided with blades 2 to 4 inches long that terminate into branched tendrils; the burnt-orange, tube-shaped blossoms, 1½ to 2 inches long, are in few-flowered, terminal clusters; the fruit is a ½- to 1-inch long, thin capsule. Cross vine is found in hammocks, swamps, thickets, and woods, and blooms from March to June, ranging from Florida to Louisiana, Illinois, Virginia and Missouri. This species is called cross vine because it has a cross-shaped pith.

HOARY PEA

(Tephrosia florida) is a slender, prostrate, purple red flowered herb of the pea family, characterized by gray hairs that lie flat on the stem and leaves. It has relatively few blossoms on long stalks that arise opposite the leaves; the flower, about ¾ inch long, is white and turns bright crimson with age. The leaves usually have thirteen segments, up to 2 inches long, that are elliptic and narrow. The pod is 1 to 2 inches long, somewhat curved, and covered with sharp, thin, straight hairs that lie flat. Look for hoary pea in the pinelands of Florida to Louisiana and North Carolina during the summer and fall.

79

red

SORREL

(Rumex hastatulus), buckwheat family, is a many-stemmed herb that grows to 2 feet tall. Each stem has long spikes of reddish flowers, which have sepals ⅛ inch long and lack petals. The spatulate leaves, 2 to 6 inches long, form a basal rosette, with a few shorter ones scattered along the stem. Fruits are tiny seeds with three papery wings. Sorrel blooms in March and April in sandy soils from Florida to Texas and Kansas and north to Massachusetts. It grows in sandy fields and along roadsides, sometimes in such dense masses in uncultivated fields that the area takes on a dull red color.

TRUMPET CREEPER

(Campsis radicans), bignonia family, has been misnamed cowitch by some who mistake the leaves for those of poison ivy. A quick look at the leaves shows the difference: poison ivy has three leaflets per leaf; trumpet creeper has seven to eleven leaflets per leaf and has no poisonous effect on the skin. The plant is a stout vine, its leaves 8 to 10 inches long with seven to eleven oval, coarsely toothed leaflets ¾ to 2 inches long. The vines lack tendrils but climb by means of aerial rootlets. The orange to red flowers, each 2 to 4 inches long, are funnel-shaped with expanded five-lobed margins; blossoms appear from early summer until fall and can be seen along highway fencerows and in woods and thickets from Florida to Texas, Missouri, New Jersey, and Michigan.

80
red

CORAL or TRUMPET HONEYSUCKLE

(Lonicera sempervirens), honeysuckle family, an evergreen twining vine, climbs up to 12 or more feet. The upper opposite leaves are fused around the stem; lower leaves, 1 to 3½ inches long, may be narrow or broad and are covered with a waxy bloom. Just above the upper leaves coral or reddish trumpet-shaped flowers up to 2 inches long appear; the inside of the trumpet is yellowish and sometimes the flower is yellow throughout. Berries are red or orange, usually clustered. The vine blooms in spring—look for it in thickets, fencerows, and along swamp edges from peninsular Florida to Texas, Nebraska, and Connecticut.

CHINA BERRY

(Melia azedarach), mahogany family, forms a rounded tree up to 45 feet tall with huge, shiny, green, much-divided, drooping leaves that fall in the winter. The leaves are 1 to 2 feet long, twice-compound, and glisten in the sunlight; the delicate, lavender, fragrant flowers form hanging clusters up to 1 foot long; and the globose fruits are ½ to 1 inch in diameter, soft, yellow, and hang in scattered clusters. China berry grows in thickets and old fields, blossoms in the spring, and ranges from Florida to Texas, Oklahoma, and North Carolina. It is an excellent shade tree and is extensively cultivated.

SODA APPLE

(Solanum ciliatum), nightshade family, is a perennial herb, up to 3 feet tall, that has erect yellow prickles on its stems, leaves, and calyx. The leaves, mostly 3 to 6 inches long, may be ovate, almost round, or angled; the white flowers are about ½ inch wide and occur in few-flowered clusters. The orange or red berry is 1 inch or more in diameter. Soda apple blooms from spring to fall in waste places and sandy soil from Florida to Texas, North Carolina, and tropical America.

ROSE VERVAIN *(Verbena tenuisecta)*, verbena family, is a colorful, low-spreading herb with highly divided, hairy leaves and rose purple, terminal clusters of flowers. The leaves are 1 to 3 inches long, toothed or lobed with the lobes themselves often toothed; the showy, tubular flowers may be up to 1 inch in diameter; and the fruit is about ⅛ inch long and one-seeded. A clump of rose vervain creates a splash of bright color along roadsides of the northern half of Florida where it grows in sandy or rocky open areas; the plants bloom from April to October in prairies, along roadsides, and in thickets from Florida to Texas, Illinois, and Vermont.

82
purple

BLAZING STAR
(Liatris chapmanii), aster family, is a downy plant, 1½ to 3 feet tall, with usually long, terminal, round spikes of very dense rose purple flowers, ¼ to ⅜ inch long. The basal, linear, finely resinous-pitted leaves are 3 to 6 inches long and 2/5 inch wide, reduced on the stem; the pappus is of 1 to 2 rows of barbed bristles, while the dry, one-seeded fruit is ⅛ to less than ¼ inch long. Blazing star blooms in summer and fall in dry pinelands and low ground from Florida to Louisiana and Texas.

CARPHEPHORUS

(Carphephorus corymbosus), aster family, is 1 to 3 feet tall with flattish heads of tubular rose-colored flowers that stand on long stalks at the tips of the stems. The flowers are enclosed by broad overlapping bracts, while the pappus is of hair-like bristles. The pale green, clasping, smooth-edged, hairy leaves, 1 to 4 inches long, are somewhat spatula-shaped at the base of the stem; they become progressively smaller on the upper stem where they become linear and do not clasp the stem. The dry, one-seeded fruit is 1/16 inch long and has ten ribs. Carphephorus grows in pinelands and blooms from July to September; it may be found along the coastal plain from Florida to Georgia and North Carolina.

LOOSESTRIFE *(Lythrum alatum)*, loosestrife family, is a much-branched, smooth herb up to 3 feet tall. It bears purplish flowers of five or six petals, ¼ inch long, in the leaf axils on the upper part of the stems. The lance to lance-ovate leaves are ½ inch long, narrowed at the base; those of the branches tend to be more crowded and more narrow. The capsule, about ¼ inch long, is enclosed in the four-toothed calyx. Loosestrife grows in low, sandy grounds and swamps from Florida to Louisiana, Texas, and Virginia. It blooms in the summer.

PURPLE VIOLET *(Viola septemloba)*, violet family, has dark violet flowers, 1 inch across, on the ends of long stalks—a distinguishing feature is a beard on the lower petal. The early leaves are entire, but the later ones are variously lobed. The fruit is a green capsule about ½ inch long that contains many tiny dark brown seeds. Purple violet grows in wet or dry pinelands, along road shoulders and cleared power line rights-of-way; it blooms from February to April and ranges from Florida to Mississippi and Virginia.

SKULLCAP
(Scutellaria integrifolia), mint family, is a perennial herb, 6 to 18 inches tall, with blue flowers, 1 inch long, arranged along the upper stem. Skullcaps are identified by the crest or bump on the top of the two-lipped, bell-shaped calyx, whose upper lip is arched. The lower leaves, 1 inch long, are stalked, broad, and tooth-ed, the upper leaves being narrow. Unlike other members of the mint family, skullcaps are not aromatic. The plants bloom from spring to fall in pinewoods and along roadsides from Florida to Texas, Ohio, and Massachusetts.

PINE HYACINTH

(Clematis baldwinii), is an herb of the buttercup family whose flowers are followed by long, feathery, gray plumes. The plant, which may grow to 18 inches tall, has few branches. The opposite leaves are 1 to 4 inches long, the lower ones being entire and the upper ones variously cleft; the flowers are solitary and lack petals but the four sepals, about 1 to 2 inches long, form bluish purple bells at the ends of the stems. The seed is about ¼ inch long and is enclosed by a feathery style up to 4 inches long. Pine hyacinths bloom in winter and spring in pinelands and damp prairies. They are limited (endemic) to peninsular Florida.

FALSE FOXGLOVE *(Agalinis fasciculata),* snapdragon family, is an erect, woody, annual 3 feet or more tall with angled, branched, rough stems. Leaves are about 1 inch long, narrow and rough and clustered in axils (fascicled). The pink purple flowers, about 1 inch long, are arranged along the stem on short stalks; each flower is broadly funnel-shaped, with five spreading lobes and a dark-spotted throat that shows some yellow in it. The nearly globose capsule is 1/5 inch long. False foxglove blooms from spring to fall in low grounds and along borders of marshes from Florida to Texas and Maryland.

BLUE TOADFLAX *(Linaria canadensis),* snapdragon family, has many stems from one root; these lie on the ground for one-third their length, then arch upward about 1 foot. Leaves, ½ to 1½ inches long, are slender, whorled or opposite. The flowers, ½ inch or less long, are pale to dark blue and located on the upper half of the stems; the blossom has five-lobed petals and four stamens. The fruit is an ⅛ inch long capsule. Blue toadflax grows in sandy soil in neglected fields and road shoulders and along ditches; it blooms from March to June with a range of Florida to Massachusetts, west to the Pacific Ocean and south to Mexico. Although rated as a weed it can form an extensive patch of blue in an otherwise ugly abandoned area.

86
purple

GARBERIA

(Garberia heterophylla), aster family, is a much-branched shrub 3 to 6 feet tall. The leaves are ¾ to 1¾ inches long, leathery, smooth-edged, broadening upward and gray green; the light purple or pink flowers are produced in terminal, somewhat flattened clusters, 3 to 4 inches wide. The brown fruit is 1 inch long, spindle-shaped, and topped with a mass of hair-like bristles. Garberia grows in dry, sandy soil in association with pines and rosemary on old coastal dunes, and blooms from spring to fall. Showy masses of the blossoms appear in late spring along the highways on the woods' edges of the coastal roads of peninsular Florida.

PRAIRIE IRIS

(Iris hexagona var. *savannarum),* iris family, has deep violet sepals with yellow crests and smaller petals of the same color. The stems reach 4 feet in height, and the flowers rise well above the tapering, sword-shaped leaves. The leaves, up to 2 feet tall, are light green, parallel veined, and interclasping; the flowers have sepals 2 to 3 inches long that curve downward and petals 2 inches long, narrower than the sepals but equally colorful. The 3- to 4-inch fruits are six-ridged capsules that taper to both ends. Prairie iris blooms in spring, the wetter seasons producing many more flowers. It is limited to the low pinelands, prairies, and cypress swamps of peninsular Florida. Look for it in the wet ditches of roadsides in central Florida.

FRAGRANT BACOPA *(Bacopa caroliniana),* snapdragon family, is a small creeping or floating herb with nearly round, clasping, aromatic, opposite leaves up to 1 inch long. The stems are smooth at the base but become covered with dense, soft, long hairs toward the top; the blue, bell-shaped flowers are 2/5 inch long and are solitary in the leaf axils. Fruit is a capsule, ¼ inch long, with dark gray brown seeds. Fragrant bacopa blooms throughout the year and can be found along muddy shores of ponds or streams or floating in the water. It ranges from Florida to Texas and Virginia.

87

purple

WILD PETUNIA

(Ruellia caroliniensis), acanthus family, is an erect herb up to 3 feet tall with simple or many-branched stems. Axillary, and with almost no stalks, the five-lobed, trumpet-shaped, lavender flowers are between 1 to 2 inches long; leaves, 1 to 4 inches long, include every variety of leaf shape and degree of hairiness. The capsule is up to ½ inch long. Wild petunia grows in dry places such as prairies, open woods, and along rocky banks and blooms all year from Florida to Texas and north to New Jersey and Indiana.

88

purple

FLORIDA VIOLET *(Viola affinis)*, violet family, is a low herb with basal, heart-shaped, pointed leaf blades, 1 inch wide, on long stalks. The solitary, pale blue flowers are at the ends of long stalks that extend above the leaves; those flowers that lack petals are concealed beneath the soil or dead leaves. They are self-fertilizing and produce the fruits and seeds. A second set of leaves, twice as large as the first, appear after the petaled flowers have matured. The fruit is a reddish brown capsule ½ inch long that contains about sixty seeds. The showy blossoms appear in early spring. This violet ranges from Florida to Louisiana and north to Wisconsin and Massachusetts in moist woods.

GROUND CHERRY *(Physalis angulata)*, nightshade family, is an annual herb with angled, hairless stems up to 3 feet tall. The oval-shaped leaves are 2 to 2¾ inches long, with wavy edges and sharp-pointed teeth; the yellow flowers, ¼ to ½ inch long, are single, axillary, smooth, and have purplish anthers. A characteristic feature is the inflated, purple-lined sac containing a yellow tomatolike fruit. Growing in rich soils, fields, pastures, and along roadsides, ground cherry blooms all year, or until frost, throughout the coastal plains of Florida, Texas, Virginia, and tropical America. It is related to the cultivated house plant Jerusalem cherry.

89

purple

GLADES LOBELIA
(Lobelia glandulosa), bluebell family, one of our common perennial lobelias, has a slender, often zigzag stem that reaches 1 to 4 feet in height. The narrow or lance-shaped lower leaves are 2 to 6 inches long, the upper leaves shorter. The flowers, 1 inch long, are blue with a white eye and are usually all on one side of the stem; the calyx is five-lobed and grandular-toothed. This lobelia blooms throughout the year in glades, wet pinelands, and bogs on the coastal plain from Florida to Virginia. Its sap is milky or colored and somewhat poisonous.

SKY-FLOWER *(Hydrolea corymbosum)*, waterleaf family, is a perennial herb, up to 2 feet tall, with smooth stems. The oval to lance-shaped leaves are 1 to 2 inches long with no stalks; the intensely azure blue flowers are ½ to ¾ inch wide in flat-topped clusters at the top of the plant. The capsule is less than ¼ inch long. Sky-flower blooms in spring and summer in wet places along the coastal plain from Florida to South Carolina.

90

purple

PICKERELWEED

(Pontederia cordata), pickerelweed family, is an aquatic herb that grows up to 3 feet tall along freshwater streams, swamps, ditches, and marshes in moist soil or shallow water. The leaves are usually 2 to 4 inches wide, are stiffly erect, and vary from lance-shaped to heart-shaped; the flowers are violet blue in dense spikes growing about a foot above the water, while the one-seeded fruits are bladderlike with a rough surface. Typically, southern pickerelweed grows in moist areas throughout Florida, west to Texas and north to Virginia. It may clog ditches and interfere with drainage. In Florida it blooms from February to December.

VIOLET BUTTERWORT

(Pinguicula caerulea), bladderwort family, is an insect-catching perennial herb, 8 inches tall, whose leaves, 1 to 2 inches long, are sticky and overlap to form a compact basal rosette. Its blue violet flowers, about 1 inch wide, grow from the ends of the stems; the flower had the characteristic butterwort spur and five irregular petal lobes. The fruit is a capsule that opens in an irregular manner. Violet butterwort blooms from March to mid-June from Florida to Louisiana and North Carolina; look for it in low pinelands and wet fields and along roadside ditches.

WATER HYACINTH *(Eichhornia crassipes),* pickerelweed family, with its beautiful lilac-shaded flowers either floats or anchors in mud. The flower stalks are 4 to 15 inches tall and the flowers, 1 to 2 inches wide, have yellow inner parts. Leaves are rounded, 1 to 3 inches wide. The leaf stalk is inflated, enabling the plant to float, roots hanging freely in the water; however, when it anchors in mud the leaf stalk elongates, losing its inflation. Fruit is a capsule usually covered with the remains of dead flowers. This plant blooms from early spring to late fall, and a large expanse of the beautiful flowers is a sight not soon forgotten. Water hyacinth has become troublesome because the floating plants clog waterways. Controls include using them as a cattle food and introducing white amur fish to feed on them; the plants are also a favorite food of the manatee. Water hyacinth was introduced from South America   and is said to have been the royal flower of the king of Siam. Presently it ranges from South America to Florida to Virginia.

PENNYROYAL *(Pilophlebis rigida),* mint family, is a shrubby mint with small, light purple flowers in dense, cylindrical spikes, 1 inch long. The stems are woody, partly reclining and partly erect, with evergreen, needlelike leaves. Leaves are about ½ inch long, numerous, and narrow; fruits are four tiny nutlets. Pennyroyal grows abundantly in sandy pinelands and blooms all year. It has a minty odor.

BACOPA *(Bacopa monnieri),* snapdragon family, is a smooth, fleshy-stemmed, creeping herb that may form dense mats of vegetation in wet depressions. It has white or pinkish white bell-shaped flowers, ⅜ to ¾ inch long, one per leaf axil; the stalkless leaves, ½ inch long, are elliptic, egg- or spatula-shaped. Fruit is a capsule, about ⅛ inch long, with gray brown seeds. Bacopa grows in moist soils along ponds and streams of the coastal plains of Florida, Texas, and Virginia, and blooms from April to November.

BAY LOBELIA *(Lobelia feayana)*, bluebell family, is a small, erect, perennial herb up to 1 foot tall. A peculiarity of all lobelias is that the upper lip is split, each half ending in a pointed lobe in front; and through the split a column of joined stamens emerges. A beard or tuft of hairs is found at the tip of the column. Bay lobelia's blue flower, about 2/5 inch long, has a white eye with two green projections at the base of the lower lip. This tiny plant grows so thickly on damp roadsides and highway medians that it creates solid masses of blue. The leaves are ½ inch long and as broad; fruits are tiny capsules. The plant blooms in damp soil from February to October, and is limited to the state of Florida.

93

pale blue

DAYFLOWER *(Commelina erecta)*, spiderwort family, is a tender, reclining plant with a conspicuous bluish flower that wilts by midmorning. The long, narrow, pointed leaves, 1 to 5 inches long, have a few hairs around their clasping bases. The upper kidney-shaped petals are 1 inch wide and deep blue, with the third petal below them being tiny and whitish. The three yellow stamens stand out noticeably against the upper petals, while two green sepals below form a half-crescent partially enclosing the lower petal. The fruit is a capsule about ⅛ inch long. Dayflowers grow in open pinelands, white sand areas, and recently culti-vated fields, and bloom from February to November. They range from Florida to Texas and north to New York.

BLUE-EYED GRASS *(Sisyrinchium atlanticum)*, iris family, has tufts of leaves up to 2 feet tall emerging from short, hard, underground stems with fibrous roots. The flattened two-edged stems bear terminal clusters of blue, six-petaled flowers, which are about ½ inch across and have a cluster of three yellow anthers in the center. Leaves are about ¼ inch wide and basal. The fruit is a capsule 1/16 inch in diameter. Blue-eyed grass is found abundantly along road shoulders and in damp fields and meadows; it blooms from March to July in damp areas from Florida to Maine. Other species of blue-eyed grasses have similar flowers but may differ in intensity of blue.

LYRE-LEAVED SAGE
(Salvia lyrata), mint family, has mostly basal, lobed or divided lyre-shaped leaves, 3 to 8 inches long, that form a basal, winter rosette from which grows a naked stem up to 2 feet tall. The leaves are often purple-shaded. The bluish purple flowers, 1 inch long, occur in several whorls along the stem. All Salvias have the pollination device of two curved stamens with filaments fastened at the middle; when an insect enters the flower the stamens are rocked forward, scattering pollen over the insect's head to be carried to the next flower. The nutlets are tiny, smooth, and egg-shaped. This plant blooms from early spring to fall in sandy, shaded areas from Florida to Texas, Connecticut, and Missouri.

Index

96

index